PRAYERS FOR THE CHURCH YEAR

GLIMPSES
OF GLORY

DAVID ADAM

D0733893

MOREHOUSE PUBLISHING
HARRISBURG, PENNSYLVANIA

First published in Great Britain in 2000 by
The Society for Promoting Christian Knowledge (SPCK)

Morehouse Publishing
P.O. Box 1321
Harrisburg, PA 17105

Printed in Great Britain

First Edition   1 3 5 7 9 10 8 6 4 2

ISBN 0-8192-1865-0

Cataloging-in-Publication Data is available from the Library of Congress.

Cover design by Laurie Westhafer

Contents

Introduction	1
ADVENT	5
CHRISTMAS	14
EPIPHANY	21
ORDINARY TIME	33
LENT	45
EASTER	59
Ascension	73
Pentecost	78
ORDINARY TIME	81
Bible Sunday	138
Dedication Festival	141
All Saints' Day	144
SUNDAYS BEFORE ADVENT	146
Christ the King	153

David Adam was born in Alnwick, Northumberland, and is now the Vicar of Holy Island. He was Vicar of Danby in North Yorkshire for over twenty years, where he discovered a gift for composing prayers in the Celtic pattern. His first book of these, *The Edge of Glory*, achieved immediate popularity, and he has since published several collections of prayers and meditations based on the Celtic tradition. His books have been translated into various languages, including Finnish and German, and have appeared as American editions.

Introduction

I love misty days when the sun suddenly breaks through; sometimes I have purposely driven high into the hills to rise out of the fog, knowing that it is low-lying fog and it can be overcome. At the moment you nearly come out of the fog it takes on a strange brightness, a luminosity that promises something different. Then suddenly you are in a land of brightness and everything seems to be bathed in a new glory: sometimes it is as if the world is being totally renewed in colour and splendour, and we see creation taking place.

On Holy Island the main windows of our house face the west and the sunsets. On some cloudy days the sun manages at sunset to drop beneath the clouds and flood the land with light, every pool and bend in the river picks up that light in a reflected glory. It is then good to stop whatever you are doing for a few moments and let that glory enter you also. Occasionally I have to climb a small hill to see the reflected light better; I have to turn aside from what I am doing and take note of what is going on around me; I have to make an effort to behold the glory. Glory does suddenly break into our lives, yet we have to make the effort to see and experience it. R. S. Thomas speaks of this experience of glory in his poem 'The Bright Field':

> I have seen the sun break through
> to illuminate a small field
> for a while, and gone my way
> and forgotten it. But that was the pearl

of great price, the one field that had
the treasure in it. I realize now
that I must give all that I have
to possess it. Life is not hurrying...

on to a receding future, nor hankering after
an imagined past. It is the turning
aside like Moses to the miracle
of the lit bush: to a brightness
that seemed as transitory as your youth
once, but is the eternity that awaits you.
   (R. S. Thomas, *Collected Poems 1945–1990*,
   Phoenix Giant, p. 302)

Life is not hurrying, and yet we seem to speed from one thing to
another and never stay long in one place. We have little time to
soak up the atmosphere and are in danger of letting the glory
pass by, or we bypass it ourselves. If we are to get glory into our
lives we have to learn to travel and to see a new way, and that
includes looking at ourselves in wonder and awe: we need to
know the Divine is within us in all his glory. In his *Confessions*,
Augustine complains:

Men go abroad to wonder at the height of the mountains,
at the huge waves of the sea,
at the long courses of the rivers,
at the vast compass of the ocean,
at the circular motion of the stars:
and they pass by themselves without wondering.
   (*Confessions*, Book X, 8.15)

Too often we are found collecting more information, or video
recordings, when we could be allowing the glory to break into
our lives. We are offered glimpse after glimpse of glory and yet
we fail to see: it is as if our hearts are hardened and our eyes are
blind. We do not create glory, it is all about us, we need to open
ourselves to it. God's world is full of his glory, he is ever present
and within it. The world and all who live upon it are in the

heart of God and God is within the heart of every piece of his creation. If you have not experienced this it is because you have not looked deep enough or long enough.

Intercession is a good way to bring to God all that is in your heart, knowing it is already in his heart, so your heart and his heart are one, you abide in him and he abides in you. Often intercession is an opening of our heart to God and so getting a glimpse of glory. I believe that deep intercession begins in the heart. Go out from your prayer knowing that God is in your heart and in the hearts of all that you meet: return to your prayers with all that you have met and experienced in your heart to be joined to the heart of God. It is amazing how many situations are suddenly washed with a new brightness when we know that God is there and that God cares. Intercession is a method of stopping and getting glimpses of the hidden glory of God.

This book is to help you rise above the gloom and enter into glory. It is not a running away from reality but seeing that there is a greater depth to reality than we normally notice or feel. It is written for you to use at home or at church and so enrich your own prayers. I would hope that each week you follow the suggestions from the Bible readings and extend your own prayers. The readings at the head of each Sunday are from the Common Worship Lectionary as used by the Church of England, the Scottish Episcopal Church, the Church in Wales, and other churches within the Anglican Communion. This is very close to the Common Lectionary of the Roman Catholic Church, and is used by other denominations. The Lectionary is designed as a three-year cycle and this book is for use with the third year, designated as Year C; *Clouds and Glory* is for Year A and *Traces of Glory* for Year B. In each book, for each Sunday, I have written a collect, that is, a prayer to collect and centre our thoughts, a list of intercessions, an offering of the peace and a blessing. As each week stands it could be used for a short service in a house group or in your home. The intercessions follow the pattern of many books of prayer: we pray, in order, for the church, the world, our homes and loved ones, the sick and the needy, and remember the saints and the departed. If you add the readings from the Lectionary to the prayers, spending some time in quiet and meditation, it will transform your worship at home and in church, and will transform you also. Use this book as a means of opening up to the presence. May God give you a glimpse of glory.

Advent

The First Sunday of Advent

Jeremiah 33. 14–16 : Ps. 25. 1–10 : 1 Thessalonians 3. 9–13 : Luke 21. 25–36

Come, Lord God, change us and we shall be changed.
Come, increase our awareness of your presence.
Come, strengthen our love for you.
Come, fill our hearts with holiness.
Come, awaken us to be ready and watchful for your coming.
Come, Lord God, change us and we shall be changed;
through him who lives and reigns with you and the Holy Spirit,
one God, now and for ever. **Amen.**

Holy and Mighty God, we long for you and your love.
Fill your Church with your grace and goodness,
that we may grow in holiness and in hospitality,
that we may reach out in mission and love,
that we may reveal your light and your glory.
Lord, make us active in service and joyful in praise.
Lord, show us your way
and teach us your paths.

We pray for the nations of the world and for righteous dealings.
May the resources of the earth be neither hoarded nor squandered,
　　but used to the benefit of all and the relief of those who need.

Strengthen all who strive for justice and integrity in world trade;
may vulnerable peoples be freed from oppression and abuse.
May we all have compassion and concern for the poor.
Lord, show us your way
and teach us your paths.

Come, Lord, fill our homes with your light and love.
Make us sensitive in our dealings and gentle in our actions.
Keep us alert to the needs and hopes of others,
that our homes may reflect your presence and your glory.
Lord, show us your way
and teach us your paths.

God of freedom and peace, we remember before you all who
    are captives to sin, vice or addiction, all who are damaged by
    oppression, violence or abuse ....
We pray also for friends and loved ones who are ill,
    especially ....
Bless all who seek to rescue and restore those who are in need
    or distress.
Lord, show us your way
and teach us your paths.

We give thanks for all who have passed beyond trouble and
    darkness and are now at peace in your kingdom.
We rejoice in the fellowship of the saints and pray we may
    follow their way of holiness and love.
Lord, show us your way
and teach us your paths.

THE PEACE

The Holy One comes to you in peace and love, that you may
increase and abound in love.
The peace of the Lord be always with you
and also with you.

6

Put off the works of darkness, put on the armour of light.
Know that God comes to you in power and in peace.
Be steadfast in your hope that the Lord may find you ready at
his coming;
and the blessing of God Almighty, the Father, the Son and the
Holy Spirit be among you and remain with you always. **Amen.**

The Second Sunday of Advent

Baruch 5. 1–9 *or* Malachi 3. 1–4 : Benedictus : Philippians 1. 3–11 : Luke 3. 1–6

Holy God, we look for you, we long for you.
Let us see that you come among us;
make us aware of your presence
and grant us a glimpse of glory;
through Jesus Christ our Lord,
who lives and reigns with you and the Holy Spirit,
one God, now and for ever. **Amen.**

Good and gracious God, we give you thanks for all who have
   told us of your love and your presence among us.
We give thanks for John the Baptist preparing the way for our
   Saviour.
We give thanks for the Apostles and Evangelists.
Mighty God, guide and empower all preachers of the word and
   ministers of the sacraments.
Bless all who proclaim your love and glory through the arts,
   music, broadcasting and publishing, all who prepare hearts
   and minds for your coming.

7

Blessed Lord, hear us
and set your people free.

Lord of freedom and grace, we pray for all held prisoner by
tyranny and oppression, all whose eyes are blind to your
glory and deaf to your word.
We remember all who do not know or love you, all whose lives
are darkened by fear.
Blessed Lord, hear us
and set your people free.

We give thanks for all who taught us the faith and led us to you,
for all who have given us a glimpse of your glory.
We pray for teachers and Sunday school teachers, for families,
friends and all who are dear to us.
We remember any who are having special difficulties or troubles
at this time.
Blessed Lord, hear us
and set your people free.

Lord of love, we pray for all who are consumed with hatred,
all who do not know how to accept or receive forgiveness,
all who are not at peace with themselves or the world.
We remember all who are anxious and fearful at this time.
We pray for all who are weakened by illness or incapacity,
especially ....
Blessed Lord, hear us
and set your people free.

Lord of glory, you destroy the darkness of the shadow of death
and open the kingdom of heaven to your loved ones.
We pray for the departed, that in your love they may rejoice in
peace.
Blessed Lord, hear us
and set your people free.

Know in your life the love of God, the forgiveness of sins and
the joy of salvation.
The peace of the Lord be always with you
and also with you.

THE BLESSING

The love and light of God scatter the darkness from before you
and guide your feet into the way of peace; and the blessing...

The Third Sunday of Advent

Zephaniah 3. 14–20 : Isaiah 12. 2–6 (or Ps. 146. 5–10) : Philippians 4. 4–7 :
Luke 3. 7–18

Good and gracious God, grant us a glimpse of your glory,
    that we may rejoice in your presence and abide in your peace;
    through Jesus Christ our Lord, who is alive and reigns with
    you and the Holy Spirit, one God, now and for ever. **Amen.**

Loving Lord, help us to know that we dwell in you and you are
    in us.
It is you, Lord, that seek out the straying and the lost:
you desire to deliver all who are in trouble,
you set out to rescue all who are oppressed,
you come to us now and seek to bring us home.
We rejoice in your presence and your almighty power.
May your church share in your healing and saving power.

We pray for the church working in areas of violence and
   rejection,
for all Christians who are persecuted for their faith.
Lord, you are our deliverer.
You are our refuge and our strength.

We pray for areas of our world where people are devalued and
   discarded:
for all who are outcasts and all who suffer from ethnic violence
   and prejudice.
We pray that the rich and those in authority may bring relief
   and hope to the poor.
We pray for all who are involved in tax-collecting and in the use
   of our taxes,
for all who are in the armed forces, and for all who maintain
   peace and order.
Lord, you are our deliverer.
You are our refuge and our strength.

Lord, we rejoice that you are with us in our homes.
Make us sensitive in our dealings with each other,
attentive to the needs and desires of our loved ones.
We pray for all homes where there is fear and abuse.
Lord, you are our deliverer.
You are our refuge and our strength.

Mighty God, you are our strength.
We pray for all who are frail and fearful, all who are weary and
   weak, all who are in pain or suffering hurt,
      especially ....
We remember all who are captives to evil and vice.
Lord, you are our deliverer.
You are our refuge and our strength.

We rejoice with all who have left the troubles of this world and
   now experience the glorious liberty of the children of God.
We pray for loved ones departed,
      especially ....

Lord, you are our deliverer.
You are our refuge and our strength.

THE PEACE

Let God's presence and peace in Christ Jesus keep a watch over
your heart and mind and free you from being anxious.
The peace of the Lord be always with you
and also with you.

THE BLESSING

Rejoice in the presence and power of God.
Be strong in the Lord and in the power of his might.
Know that the Lord is at hand.
And the blessing...

The Fourth Sunday of Advent

Micah 5. 2–5a : Magnificat *or* Ps. 80. 1–7 : Hebrews 10. 5–10 :
Luke 1. 39–45 [46–55]

Lord our Saviour, our hope is in you:
no one is beyond your love,
no one is beyond your saving power.
Give us grace to recognize you and welcome you
as you come to us;
through Jesus Christ our Lord,

11

who is alive and reigns with you and the Holy Spirit,
one God, now and for ever. **Amen.**

Lord, open our eyes that we may behold your glory,
open our minds to know that you are with us,
open our hearts to the love that you give us.
We give thanks that in Christ you share in our humanity and
open for us the gate of glory.
We pray for the church's work among children, in nurseries, in
schools and in church.
We pray for those who seek to proclaim the sacredness of all
life.
Give your church the courage to proclaim that you come among
us.
God of love, God of glory,
be known among us.

We pray for all who seek to support family life, all who care for
homeless or unwanted children, all children taken into care.
We remember the street children of the world and all who are
used as cheap labour.
Bless the work of the Children's Society and the NSPCC.
God of love, God of glory,
be known among us.

We rejoice in the love of our homes.
We pray for all who have enriched our lives by their goodness,
all who have accepted us and cared for us.
We pray for all who are separated from loved ones at this time,
all who are lonely.
We remember all who will come together for Christmas as
families and all who are alone.
God of love, God of glory,
be known among us.

We pray for all who are hungry for acceptance,
who are hungry for love,

all who long to be needed.
We remember all who are in hospital and loved ones who are
   anxious.
We pray especially for ....
God of love, God of glory,
be known among us.

Lord God, you came to earth that in your power and love we
   might ascend into heaven, bless our friends and loved ones
   who are departed this life with the gift of life and love
   eternal.
God of love, God of glory,
be known among us.

THE PEACE

Our Lord comes to us in power and in glory.
Our Lord seeks to abide with us always.
The peace of the Lord be always with you
and also with you.

THE BLESSING

The power and peace of the presence fill your life and your
home.
The God of hope fill you with all joy and peace in believing.
And the blessing ...

Christmas

Christmas Day

Any of these sets of readings may be used on the evening of Christmas Eve and on Christmas Day.

I	II	III
Isaiah 9. 2–7	Isaiah 62. 6–12	Isaiah 52. 7–10
Ps. 96	Ps. 97	Ps. 98
Titus 2. 11–14	Titus 3. 4–7	Hebrews 1. 1–4 [5–12]
Luke 2. 1–14 [15–20]	Luke 2. [1–7] 8–20	John 1. 1–14

Almighty Father, we rejoice in the coming of Christ our Lord. We pray that, as he has taken on our humanity, through your grace and goodness we may share in your divinity, and so partake in the radiance of your glory; through him who came down for us and is alive and reigns with you and the Holy Spirit, one God, now and for ever. **Amen.**

Holy and lowly One, Jesus, Friend and Brother,
we rejoice in your coming among us.
You come down to lift us up.
You come as the Light to our darkness:
we welcome and adore you.
We pray for your church throughout the world;
may we reveal your saving power and abide in your love.
We pray for the work of the church among the poor and the
　outcasts of our world.

14

King of glory, come to earth.
Lift us up into your kingdom.

Prince of Peace, we pray for the peace of Jerusalem, for peace
in the Holy Land;
for peace among nations and goodwill throughout this world;
for the communities to which we belong and the places where
we work,
that they may know your presence and your peace.
King of glory, come to earth.
Lift us up into your kingdom.

Lord, born at Bethlehem, we pray for our families,
for all with whom we will share this Christmas time:
we rejoice in their love and your love for us all.
We remember absent friends and loved ones,
all who will be alone this Christmas time.
King of glory, come to earth.
Lift us up into your kingdom.

At this time of joy and rejoicing, we remember all who are sad,
all whose lives are full of sorrow, fear or darkness.
We pray for all who are in care, in hospital or in a hospice;
we remember those who have no home and will sleep rough this
night.
We pray especially for friends and loved ones who are ill.
King of glory, come to earth.
Lift us up into your kingdom.

We rejoice with all who have entered into the fullness of your
presence, all who are at peace in your kingdom.
We pray for friends and loved ones departed.
King of glory, come to earth.
Lift us up into your kingdom.

This day heaven comes down, we are one with our God;
the Word is made flesh and dwells among us.
The peace of the Lord be always with you
and also with you.

The peace of Jesus Christ, the Son of God, born of the blessed
Virgin Mary, abide with you, in your heart and in your home;
and the blessing . . .

The First Sunday of Christmas

1 Samuel 2. 18–20, 26 : Ps. 148. [1–6] 7–14 : Colossians 3. 12–17 : Luke 2. 41–52

Lord of all power and might, let us not just suppose you to be in
our company, but seek you out until we find you and rejoice in
your presence; through Jesus Christ our Saviour, who lives and
reigns with you and the Holy Spirit, one God, now and for ever.
Amen.

We rejoice that we are created in your image, that we are called
    to be your sons and daughters.
May the church at all times reveal your glory and lead many to
    the glorious liberty that is for the children of God.
We pray for all who teach the faith and each of us as we are
    called to share the faith.
We pray for all who are seekers, all who long for you and for a
    glimpse of your glory.

16

Lord, we seek you and your love.
Come, be known among us.

We pray for all young people in their search for truth and
meaning, that they will not be led astray or directed in wrong
paths.
Guide and direct all who influence the minds of young people
through broadcasting, music and publishing.
We pray for young people who have left home and for parents
anxious for their well-being.
Lord, we seek you and your love.
Come, be known among us.

We give thanks for our own homes and loved ones,
for those who have sought us out when we have gone astray,
for those who accepted us even when we ignored their advice.
We pray for all families where there is tension and lack of trust,
for all who are anxious about loved ones at this time.
Lord, we seek you and your love.
Come, be known among us.

We remember those who have gone astray and cannot find their
way back.
We pray for street children and those separated from loved ones
through war.
We pray for children in care or in hospital,
for all who feel unloved or unwanted.
We remember especially any who have lost a child or a loved
one this week.
Lord, we seek you and your love.
Come, be known among us.

We rejoice that you will bring us home to your eternal kingdom
where sorrow and pain are no more.
We pray for loved ones departed.
Lord, we seek you and your love.
Come, be known among us.

Clothe yourselves with love, which binds everything together in perfect harmony.
Let the peace of Christ rule in your hearts.
The peace of the Lord be always with you
and also with you.

THE BLESSING

Whatever you do, in word or deed, do everything in the name of the Lord Jesus, giving thanks to God the Father through him; and the blessing...

The Second Sunday of Christmas

Jeremiah 31. 7–14 : Ps. 147. 12–20 : *Or*: Ecclus. 24. 1–12 : *Canticle*: Wisdom of Solomon 10. 15–21 : Ephesians 1. 3–14 : John 1. [1–9] 10–18

Eternal light, scatter the darkness from our hearts and minds; enlighten our lives with your glory, and give us the power and wisdom to live as sons and daughters of God; through Jesus Christ our Lord, who is alive and reigns with you, O Father, and the Holy Spirit, one God, now and for ever. **Amen.**

Mighty God, empower all who seek you to find you:
may your church proclaim your saving power, reveal your
    eternal love, and abide in your peace.
We pray for all who seek to live out their faith in their daily
    lives, all who stand for justice, freedom and unity.

Lord of light and love,
save your people.

We give thanks for all scientists and inventors.
We pray for all who influence our lives by their experiments and
discoveries, that they may work with wisdom and sensitivity.
For all who are in positions of power and authority, all leaders
of nations, governments and decision-makers.
We pray for all who work in dangerous places, whose lives are
at risk as they care for others.
We pray for the emergency services.
Lord of light and love,
save your people.

We give you thanks for all who have cared for us and protected
us:
we pray especially for our own homes and loved ones.
We remember all who are facing poverty or homelessness at this
time.
Lord of light and love,
save your people.

Lord of might and love, we come to you with all who are ill.
We remember today all who have been ill for a long time, all
who are disabled, all whose sickness has no cure.
We pray for all who will go into hospital this week, all who will
undergo operations.
Lord of light and love,
save your people.

We give thanks for all who have passed through the waters of
death and are now in the fullness of your kingdom.
We pray for loved ones departed and for all who built up our
communities.
Lord of light and love,
save your people.

19

In him we have redemption and the forgiveness of sins
     according to the riches of his grace.
The peace of the Lord be always with you
and also with you.

THE BLESSING

The God of grace who called you into his eternal glory in Christ
Jesus support and strengthen you as you work for him; and the
blessing . . .

The Epiphany

The Epiphany

Isaiah 60. 1–6 : Ps. 72. [1–9] 10–15 : Ephesians 3. 1–12 : Matthew 2. 1–12

Lord of light and love, let the radiance of your presence be a light to our path and a guide on our journey. Banish from us all deeds of darkness, that we may come to your presence and walk before you as children of light; through him who is the light of the world, Jesus Christ our Lord. **Amen.**

O God, who by the leading of the star brought people of various nations to worship before you, give guidance to all who are seekers, all reaching out to extend their vision and their lives.
We pray for all pilgrims and those who are seeking to deepen their faith.
Grant that your church may be welcoming and sensitive to all who are looking for meaning and purpose.
We pray especially for all who teach and preach about you and your love.
We pray for those who do not know or love you, and for the mission of our church.
Lord, come into the world.
Lighten our darkness.

We pray for nations that are emerging into a new freedom or
   awareness.
We remember countries where people are oppressed or suffer
   tyranny.
We pray especially for those recovering from war or from
   disasters.
O Lord, bless the work of relief organizations and all who care
   for the poor.
We remember in our prayers all who are travellers at this time,
   all who are homeless, all who are refugees.
Lord, come into the world.
Lighten our darkness.

We give thanks, O Lord, that you are present in our homes and
   in our lives:
we seek your blessing and your guidance.
We pray for friends and loved ones, especially any in trouble or
   in need.
Bless all who through their talents and generosity have enriched
   our lives.
We pray for all who live in sordid homes or places of squalor.
Lord, come into the world.
Lighten our darkness.

Lord, we give thanks that you seek out and save the lost.
We pray for all who have lost their way, who have been
   side-tracked,
who are living below their potential or their abilities,
all whose lives are unfulfilled, all restricted by oppression or illness:
we remember the chronically ill, those in constant pain, the
   depressed and the despairing.
Lord, come into the world.
Lighten our darkness.

We pray for all who are coming to the end of their journey here
   on earth and pray that they may come into your presence and
   kingdom.

We pray for all who have come before your face and rejoice in
the fullness of life eternal.
Lord, come into the world.
Lighten our darkness.

THE PEACE

The light of Christ lead you into the way of peace.
The peace of the Lord be always with you
and also with you.

THE BLESSING

The light of the Creator shine upon you.
The light of the Saviour scatter the darkness from before you.
The light of the Spirit guide you into the fullness of glory.
And the blessing . . .

The Baptism of Christ
(The First Sunday of Epiphany)

Isaiah 43. 1–7 : Ps. 29 : Acts 8. 14–17 : Luke 3. 15–17, 21–22

Lord, you have called us. Make us worthy of our calling, that,
in the mighty name of the Father, Son and Holy Spirit, we may
rejoice in your love and saving power, and proclaim your
presence and glory in the world; through Jesus Christ our Lord,

who is alive and reigns with you, Almighty Father, and the Holy
   Spirit, one God, now and for ever. **Amen.**

Loving God, we give thanks that you have called us and that we
   belong to you.
Take us, Lord, and do with us as you desire.
Protect us from all that is evil and lead us into the ways of
   peace.
We pray for all who are being prepared for baptism or
   confirmation, for Godparents and sponsors,
for all who are seeking to immerse themselves in your presence
   and love.
Give strength to your people.
Immerse us in your presence and peace.

We seek to know your love for the world and that the world
   is in your heart.
We pray for all who are working for peace, all who are seeking
   to improve our world.
We remember all who are struggling to gain freedom and
   independence, for emerging nations and communities.
We pray especially for any who are suffering from ethnic
   violence or prejudice, for countries and peoples who are at
   war.
Give strength to your people.
Immerse us in your presence and peace.

Holy and Mighty God, enfold us in your peace:
may your presence be known, your kingdom come, in our
   hearts, in our homes and in our land.
We pray for our loved ones, especially for any who are
   distressed at this time.
Give strength to your people.
Immerse us in your presence and peace.

We remember before you all who feel unwanted or neglected:
we remember lonely people and all who have no one to care for
   them.

We pray today for those who are mentally disturbed,
all who by the nature of their illness are kept in institutions.
We pray for friends and loved ones who are
    ill . . . .
Give strength to your people.
Immerse us in your presence and peace.

We rejoice with the church triumphant and pray for loved ones
    who have entered life eternal and now rest in the love of the
    Father, the peace of the Son, and the life of the Holy Spirit.
Give strength to your people.
Immerse us in your presence and peace.

THE PEACE

God says: Do not be afraid, for I have redeemed you;
I have called you by your name, you are mine.
The peace of the Lord be always with you
and also with you.

THE BLESSING

The Father, who created you, is with you;
the Son, who redeemed you, is with you;
the Spirit, who strengthens you, is with you;
the Holy Three enfold you; and the blessing . . .

The Second Sunday of Epiphany

Isaiah 62. 1–5 : Ps. 36. 5–10 : 1 Corinthians 12. 1–11 : John 2. 1–11

Almighty and everlasting God, you give gifts to all your people:
you give us the power and ability to do what you would have
  us do.
Help us to use the gifts you have given us for the benefit of
  others and to your glory;
through Jesus Christ our Lord,
who is alive and reigns with you and the Holy Spirit,
one God, now and for ever. **Amen.**

We give thanks to you, O Lord, for all who enrich our world by
  their talents and abilities.
We pray for those with the gift of healing and for all healing
  ministries.
We pray for those who are visionaries and those who plan our
  future:
may we all exercise the gift of discernment and distinguish the
  true from the false.
We pray for all who are preparing for marriage, for all who
  have recently fallen in love.
We remember homes where there is tension or estrangement
  and all homes where there is a breakdown in marriage or in
  relationships.
Lord, come to us (who are empty)
and fill us with your love.

Lord, who has given us this world and all that is in it, help us to
use its resources properly,
that we do not waste now what should be saved for the
future:
that the resources of the sea are not over-used, that fossil fuels
are not too easily spent.
We pray that we take care not to pollute the earth or our
environment.
Bless all who are seeking to conserve and to protect our natural
resources.
We pray for countries whose crops have failed, whose harvest is
poor, and for all who live in desert places.
Lord, come to us (who are empty)
and fill us with your love.

We rejoice, O God, that you delight in us.
You will not leave us desolate: you are God who renews and
restores your creation.
We pray that we may learn to delight in each other and give our
attention and love to each other.
Bless our homes and our loved ones with your fullness;
renew and restore us in strength and in love.
We pray for all who are struggling in their relationships.
Lord, come to us (who are empty)
and fill us with your love.

We pray for all who have been made to feel inadequate or
unwanted,
for all who feel as if they have run out of energy or hope,
for all who feel empty or that life is too much for them.
We remember the despairing, the despondent, and all who feel
utterly drained.
Lord, come to us (who are empty)
and fill us with your love.

We rejoice with all who have received of your fullness in your
kingdom,

all who have been restored and renewed by your love and
   saving power.
We pray for loved ones departed,
   especially ....
Lord, come to us (who are empty)
and fill us with your love.

THE PEACE

The gift of the Spirit fills us with love, joy and peace.
The peace of the Lord be always with you
and also with you.

THE BLESSING

The Almighty God, the giver of all good gifts, fill you with joy,
peace and love; and the blessing of . . .

The Third Sunday of Epiphany

Nehemiah 8. 1–3, 5–6, 8–10 : Ps. 19. 1–6 [7–14] : 1 Corinthians 12. 12–31a :
Luke 4. 14–21

Lord, as you have called us to share in your outreach of love to
the world, fill us with the power of your Spirit, that, in your
strength and by your guidance, we may lead others to be aware
of you, and live to your praise and glory; through Jesus Christ
our Lord, who is alive and reigns with you and the Holy Spirit,
one God, now and for ever. **Amen.**

Lord of all joy, you are our hope and our strength, a very
present help in all troubles.
We give thanks for all who tell of your love by translating the
Scriptures, by preaching the word, by teaching the faith.
We pray for all who are standing up for what they believe, and
speaking out against evil and tyranny.
We remember before you all Christians who are being
persecuted for their faith: all who are oppressed, mocked,
scorned, those who are suffering through the prejudice or vested
interests of others.
Lord, renew your people
and sustain us by your mighty power.

We give thanks for all who are working for the care and
renewal of our earth.
Give guidance and courage to all who work in conservation and
ecology,
all who care for oppressed peoples and minority groups,
all who look after the lost and rejected in our world.
Give wisdom and love to all who are working for peace and
justice.
Lord, renew your people
and sustain us by your mighty power.

We give you thanks for all who have been a strength and
support to us.
We pray for the work of the Samaritans and all who guide or
counsel others.
We remember any of our loved ones who are in need.
May we always have a respect and sensitivity towards each
other.
We pray especially for any who are suffering from broken
relationships.
Lord, renew your people
and sustain us by your mighty power.

God of love, we remember before you all who feel unloved or
    neglected.
We pray for children who feel they are unwanted or rejected.
For all people who are ill and on their own, for those who have
    no one to care for them.
We remember all who have been taken into care this week.
We pray for friends who are ill, especially ....
Lord, renew your people
and sustain us by your mighty power.

We give thanks that you are the Lord who loves us and renews
    us.
We pray for loved ones departed, that they may rest in your
    love and be renewed and restored by your almighty power.
Lord, renew your people
and sustain us by your mighty power.

THE PEACE

Let the presence and joy of the Lord be your strength and peace.
The peace of the Lord be always with you
and also with you.

THE BLESSING

God strengthen you by his mighty power.
Christ protect you from all evil.
The Holy Spirit renew and refresh you.
And the blessing . . .

The Fourth Sunday of Epiphany

Ezekiel 43.27 – 44.4 : Ps. 48 : 1 Corinthians 13. 1–13 : Luke 2. 22–40

O Lord our God, you created us out of love, you redeemed us by your love, you sustain us with your love. Let the glory of your love be seen in us, that we may reflect your presence and show forth your love in the world; through Jesus Christ your Son our Lord, who is alive and reigns with you, in the unity of the Holy Spirit, one God, now and for ever. **Amen.**

Lord, your glory fills the whole world.
Open our eyes that we may have a glimpse of your glory.
We give thanks that you, O Christ, shared in our humanity that
    we might by your grace share in the Divine.
We pray that the whole church may show forth your glory.
We pray especially for preachers and prayer leaders, for junior
    church groups and Bible study meetings, for theological
    colleges and religious communities.
Lord, look upon us
and let us show forth your glory.

We pray for city planners, and all who make decisions that
    affect our future.
We remember all those who are striving to improve our world
    and make it more peaceful:
for peace-makers, for protectors of peoples, for all who keep
    our world safe.
We remember all who live in sordid dwellings or among violent
    and evil people.
We pray for all whose lives have lost any radiance.

31

Lord, look upon us
and let us show forth your glory.

We give thanks for all who have revealed your glory to us.
We pray for those who cared for us and continue to do so,
for those who have been good companions, friends and guides.
We pray for the communities to which we belong.
Lord, look upon us
and let us show forth your glory.

We pray for all who are struggling at this time, all whose lives
  are dull and whose work is boring.
We remember all who are unable to achieve what they want to
  do, through disability or illness, all who feel frustrated or
  thwarted.
We pray for all who are ill at home or in hospital.
Lord, look upon us
and let us show forth your glory.

We give thanks for all who have entered into the glory of your
  kingdom, for all who behold and share in your splendour.
We pray for loved ones departed, that they may glory in your
  love.
Lord, look upon us
and let us show forth your glory.

THE PEACE

Let the love of God fill your hearts and minds.
Let God change you and you shall be changed.
The peace of the Lord be always with you
and also with you.

THE BLESSING

God, who created you in love and for love, fill your life with his
love, increase your faith, strengthen your hope, that you may
walk before him in peace; and the blessing . . .

Ordinary Time

Proper 1

*Sunday between 3 and 9 February inclusive
(if earlier than the Second Sunday before Lent)*

———

Isaiah 6. 1–8 [9–13] : Ps. 138 : 1 Corinthians 15. 1–11 : Luke 5. 1–11

Grant, O gracious God, that we not only hear your word, but understand it and receive it into our hearts; that we not only receive it, but reveal it in our lives by living up to our calling and to your praise and glory; through Jesus Christ our Lord, who lives and reigns with you and the Holy Spirit, one God, world without end. **Amen.**

Holy God, open our ears to your call,
our eyes to your presence,
our hearts to your love.
Give us the courage to say, 'Here I am Lord, send me.'
Strengthen our faith that we may be willing at all times to heed
    your call.
We pray for all who are called to proclaim your glory,
all who seek out the lost, uplift the fallen and comfort the
    wounded.
We pray for the outreach of the church to which we belong.

Lord, as you have called us,
make us worthy of our calling.

God, as you are gracious to us, make us sensitive to the needs of
others.
We remember before you the world's poor, nations that are in
debt, hungry and homeless peoples.
We pray for all who work for relief organizations, and for the
emergency services, for all who give their lives in the care and
service of others.
Lord, as you have called us,
make us worthy of our calling.

We give you thanks for all who have encouraged us and built up
our confidence.
We pray for the young, that they may not be discouraged.
We pray for all families that are in difficulty at this time, for
young people forced to leave home.
We give thanks for our homes and all that you have called us to
do.
Lord, as you have called us,
make us worthy of our calling.

Lord of all compassion, we pray for the lost and the dis-spirited:
for all who have lost hope or vision, for those who have lost
confidence in themselves, in others or in you.
We pray for all who are anxious and fearful.
We remember all whose lives are restricted by illness or
circumstance.
Lord, as you have called us,
make us worthy of our calling.

Lord, you call us to share with you in the glory of your eternal
kingdom.
Make us worthy of our calling.
We remember all who have served you faithfully and are now in
life eternal.

Lord, as you have called us,
make us worthy of our calling.

THE PEACE

Grace, mercy and peace be yours from God who abounds in
love and calls you to his glory.
The peace of the Lord be always with you
and also with you.

THE BLESSING

The God of love who calls you,
guide you this day and always:
his might uphold you,
his love enfold you,
his peace empower you;
and the blessing . . .

Proper 2

*Sunday between 10 and 16 February inclusive
(if earlier than the Second Sunday before Lent)*

————

Jeremiah 17. 5–10 : Ps. 1 : 1 Corinthians 15. 12–20 : Luke 6. 17–26

Lord God, all power in heaven and earth belongs to you.
Shield us in times of distress and danger,
protect us from all that is evil and destructive,

renew us and refresh us that we may serve you,
and that we may proclaim your power and your glory;
through Jesus Christ our Lord,
who is alive and reigns with you and the Holy Spirit,
one God, now and for ever. **Amen.**

We give you thanks for all who seek to walk in the way of the
   Lord.
We pray for those who teach us the faith by word and by
   action.
We remember those who spend their lives in your service.
We pray for all seekers, all who do not know or love you, all
   who seek contact and who long for love.
Lord, may your church be open and welcoming to all.
Go before us, O Lord,
and guide us by your continual help.

We remember all who watch, wait and weep this day:
those who long for freedom, those who mourn because of the
   restrictions imposed upon them.
Bless all who work for peace, for liberty, for justice:
all who seek to feed the hungry and care for the poor.
Go before us, O Lord,
and guide us by your continual help.

We give thanks for our homes and loved ones.
We pray for our community and neighbourhood,
for peace and harmony in all our dealings,
that we may be aware of the needs around us and where we can
   serve.
Go before us, O Lord,
and guide us by your continual help.

We pray for the world's poor: all displaced peoples, refugees
   and those who seek political asylum;
for all who have become discouraged or despondent;
for those who have lost the will to strive and to live.

We pray for all who are ill at this time,
especially ....
We pray for doctors and nurses and all who care for the ill.
Go before us, O Lord,
and guide us by your continual help.

We remember all who have died this week, especially those
whose deaths were untimely: those who died through
accidents, violence or disasters.
May they rejoice in the fullness of life which is eternal.
Go before us, O Lord,
and guide us by your continual help.

THE PEACE

Blessed are all who put their trust in the Lord.
He will keep them in his presence and his peace.
The peace of the Lord be always with you
and also with you.

THE BLESSING

God the Father, who created you, strengthen you.
God the Son, who redeemed you, support you.
God the Holy Spirit, who guides you, direct you.
And the blessing ...

Proper 3

Sunday between 17 and 23 February inclusive
(if earlier than the Second Sunday before Lent)

———

Genesis 45. 3–11, 15 : Ps. 37. 1–7 [8–11, 39–40] : 1 Corinthians 15. 35–38, 42–50 :
Luke 6. 27–38

God of grace and glory, give us the gift of generosity, that we
may reveal your love and forgiveness, and live in fellowship and
peace with each other as we work for the coming of your
kingdom; through Jesus Christ our Lord, who is alive and
reigns with you and the Holy Spirit, one God, now and for ever.
Amen.

Lord, you are our delight and our joy,
we seek to reflect your grace and goodness:
make us slow to anger and not too ready to condemn.
We pray that your church may be open and welcoming to all in
    need.
We remember today churches that are divided by factions or
    through animosity.
We pray for churches that are working to heal divisions and
    hurts.
God of love and hope,
give us your peace.

God of peace, we pray for peace-givers and peace-makers.
We pray for all who are seeking to bring reconciliation and
    hope to communities and peoples.

We remember today the work of Amnesty International, the
  United Nations and the peace-keeping forces of the world.
We pray for peoples involved in conflict, strife, or aggression.
God of love and hope,
give us your peace.

We remember all who have hardened themselves, or become
  insensitive,
all who are afraid of being moved or touched, all afraid of close
  contact,
all who are suffering from a breakdown in relationships.
We give thanks for our homes and our loved ones and pray for
  their peace,
that we may have peace in our communities and in our lives.
God of love and hope,
give us your peace.

We remember with love all who are struggling at this time,
all who realize that they are perishable beings through illness or
  disability:
may they be strong in the spirit and strong in the Lord.
We pray for all whose lives are disturbed or distressed.
We pray especially for friends who are ill or in need.
God of love and hope,
give us your peace.

We rejoice that in our God we are more than conquerors.
In your power, O Lord, we will overcome all evil, we will
  triumph over death and rejoice in life eternal.
We pray for loved ones departed, that they may rest in peace
  and rise in glory.
God of love and hope,
give us your peace.

Fix your hearts upon God where true joys are to be found.
The peace of the Lord be always with you
and also with you.

THE BLESSING

Give love to your enemies, do good to those who hate you;
live as true sons and daughters of your heavenly Father;
and the blessing...

The Second Sunday Before Lent

Genesis 2. 4b–9, 15–25 : Ps. 65 : Revelation 4 : Luke 8. 22–25

God, you have created us out of your love
and for your love.
Christ, you have redeemed us by your love
and for your love.
Holy Spirit, you inspire us with your love
and for your love.
Give us grace to perceive your love
and to reflect your love,
Father, Son and Holy Spirit. **Amen.**

Holy God, our Creator, Redeemer and Sustainer,
you give us love, you give us life, you give us yourself.
Help us to give our lives, our love, ourselves to you, Father, Son
and Holy Spirit.

Lord, we put our trust in you amid the storms of life.
Grant that your church may seek out the perishing, the troubled and the lost;
let your church be seen to uphold the overwhelmed and the distressed.
We pray especially today for the church's work among those who cannot cope for themselves.
Mighty God, come to us
and give us your peace.

We pray for all travellers, especially today for those who work upon the sea.
We pray for all who care for our fishermen and mariners.
Lord, may we all develop a respect for your world and use its resources with care.
We pray for all who are seeking to harness the power of the wind or the sea.
Mighty God, come to us
and give us your peace.

God, grant us a glimpse of glory in our homes,
let us see that the love of our loved ones is a reflection of your love.
As we are loved and cared for, help us to care for all who are in need.
We pray for our places of work and rest, that they may be places of peace.
Mighty God, come to us
and give us your peace.

We pray for all who are or feel they are sinking amid the storms of life,
all who are in dangerous or violent surroundings,
all suffering from flood, storm, or any other natural disaster.
We pray for areas where crops have failed and homes have been destroyed.

We remember friends and loved ones who are going through a time of illness or distress.
Mighty God, come to us
and give us your peace.

Loving God, we give thanks that, as we experience our own mortality, you come to us and reach down to our need; you offer us life which is imperishable.
We pray for all who are dying at this time.
We remember loved ones departed.
Mighty God, come to us
and give us your peace.

THE PEACE

The Lord Jesus Christ, who stilled the waves and calmed the storm, uplift you and enfold you in his peace.
The peace of the Lord be always with you
and also with you.

THE BLESSING

The peace of Almighty God, the Creator, be yours.
The peace of Christ, the Prince of Peace, be yours.
The peace of the Holy Spirit, the Sustainer, be yours.
In the storms of life, the peace of the Holy Three be yours.
And the blessing . . .

42

The Sunday Next Before Lent

Exodus 34. 29–35 : Ps. 99 : 2 Corinthians 3.12 – 4.2 : Luke 9. 28–36 [37–43a]

Almighty Father, God of grace and goodness, awaken us to your glory, that our lives may reflect your radiance, that we may share in your likeness, and in walking the way of Christ our Lord may reveal your love to the world; through the same Christ our Lord, who is alive and reigns with you and the Holy Spirit, one God, now and for ever. **Amen.**

Lord, we pray that the glory of your presence may fill our lives
    and be reflected in all that we do.
We ask that our churches may be radiant with your glory, that
    the gospel is not veiled from sight but revealed in our actions
    and witness.
We pray for all preachers, for ministers of the word and the
    sacraments, that they will reveal to us the face of our Lord
    Jesus Christ.
We remember especially all who are suffering for their faith.
Lord, let your glory be about us
and fill our hearts and minds.

We give thanks for all who add beauty and glory to our world.
We pray for artists, writers, musicians and craftspeople; for
    gardeners, architects, planners and for all who influence our
    daily life.
We pray for all who live in desolate areas and places of
    deprivation.

Lord, let your glory be about us
and fill our hearts and minds.

We give thanks for all who have enriched our lives and
improved our environment.
We pray for those who work to meet our daily needs.
We ask your blessing upon our homes and places of work, upon
our friends and our loved ones.
Lord, let your glory be about us
and fill our hearts and minds.

We pray for all who are finding life dull or drab, for all who are
getting no joy or satisfaction out of their life.
We remember the stressed and the distressed, the over-worked
and the over-anxious.
We pray also for all who suffer from defective hearing or vision,
especially any who are losing the use of their faculties.
We ask for comfort and strength for all who are ill,
especially ....
Lord, let your glory be about us
and fill our hearts and minds.

Lord, we pray that we may be changed from glory to glory.
We pray for all who now see you face to face,
all who rejoice in the glory of your nearer presence.
We pray especially for ....
Lord, let your glory be about us
and fill our hearts and minds.

THE PEACE

Glory to God: on earth, peace and good will among us all.
The peace of the Lord be always with you
and also with you.

THE BLESSING

To the King, eternal, immortal, invisible, the only God, be
honour, glory and power for ever and ever; and the blessing . . .

Lent

The First Sunday of Lent

Deuteronomy 26. 1–11 : Ps. 91. 1–2, 9–16 (*or* 1–11) : Romans 10. 8b–13 :
Luke 4. 1–13

Almighty God, give us strength to stand against all that is evil:
keep us firm in the times of trial and temptation;
make us resolute in obeying your will and in seeking your
    kingdom;
give us the power to stay true to you and proclaim your
    salvation;
through Jesus Christ our Lord,
who is alive and reigns with you and the Holy Spirit,
one God, now and for ever. **Amen.**

Loving God, throughout all ages you have rescued and restored
    your people;
we come to you for refreshment and renewal.
Lord, protect us from all the terrors of the night and the dangers
    of the day.
We pray for all who are seeking to know their vocation, all who
    are trying to sort out their priorities.
We pray for all who are called to minister to others, for
    spiritual counsellors and advisers.

Lord, in you we trust.
You are our refuge and strength.

We pray for all in positions of authority, that they do not
misuse their powers;
for leaders of peoples and for all who make decisions about our
future.
We remember all who are suffering from hunger or poverty,
all who are experiencing a time of dryness or aridity in their
lives.
We pray also for all who are living below par, all who have lost
their way.
Lord, in you we trust.
You are our refuge and strength.

We give thanks for all who have provided for us and protected
us, for those who inspired us or directed us.
We pray that we may be sensitive to your call and ready to do
your will.
We ask you to bless and protect our loved ones and friends.
Lord, in you we trust.
You are our refuge and strength.

We pray for all who are caught up in crime or addiction,
for all who are wasting their lives or giving their allegiance to
wrong things.
We pray for all who regret what they have done and are full of
remorse;
may they find new hope and courage in you, O Lord.
We remember all who are ill and longing to live full lives,
for all who are restricted in any way.
We pray especially for ....
Lord, in you we trust.
You are our refuge and strength.

We give thanks for all who have escaped the temptations of the
world, the flesh and the devil and are now at peace in your
eternal kingdom.

We pray for all who have once been part of this church and
community, for the saints and all who have enriched our
world.
May they, with our dear ones departed, rejoice in doing your
will in your kingdom.
Lord, in you we trust.
You are our refuge and strength.

THE PEACE

Everyone who calls upon the name and the power of the Lord
Jesus, will come to his peace and will be saved.
The peace of the Lord be always with you
and also with you.

THE BLESSING

The Lord deliver you from all evil,
confirm and strengthen you in all goodness,
refresh you as you hunger for him;
and the blessing...

The Second Sunday of Lent

Genesis 15. 1–12, 17–18 : Ps. 27 : Philippians 3.17 – 4.1 : Luke 13. 31–35

Holy God, as you have called us, make us holy.
Shield us from all that is evil and destructive,
protect us in body and in soul;

extend our vision of our purpose and journey,
that we may know we are your people and citizens of your
    kingdom;
through Jesus Christ our Lord,
who is alive and reigns with you and the Holy Spirit,
one God, world without end. **Amen.**

Mighty God, you are a very present help in all our troubles, we
    put our trust in you.
Teach us your ways, O Lord, and show us your paths.
Guide your church, that it may lead others to behold your love
    and glory.
We pray for those who care for seekers, wanderers and the lost:
bless all who work as counsellors, Samaritans, and in marriage
    guidance.
We pray for all those who are persecuted for their faith.
Lord, we put our hope in you.
You are our protector and our shield.

Loving Father, we remember before you all who are refugees,
    all who have been driven out of their homes by violence or
    disaster.
We pray for those who have had their homes repossessed, for
    those who have never known the shelter of a home.
We ask you to guide and strengthen all who work with the
    homeless.
Lord, we put our hope in you.
You are our protector and our shield.

We give you thanks for all who have provided for us: we give
    thanks for parents and loved ones.
We ask your blessing upon our families and community, upon
    all who seek to strengthen the bonds of family life and love.
We pray for any who are suffering from a breakdown in their
    relationships.
Lord, we put our hope in you.
You are our protector and our shield.

Lord, you are our strength in times of weakness, you are our
   hope in times of darkness.
We pray for all who are struggling at this time, all who are
   finding life hard and the outlook bleak.
We remember friends and loved ones who are ill,
   especially ....
Lord, we put our hope in you.
You are our protector and our shield.

We rejoice in the hope that our earthly bodies may be changed
   and become like your glorious body.
Change us, Lord, and we shall be changed.
We pray for all our loved ones departed this life,
that they may now share in the glory that shall be revealed to
   us.
Lord, we put our hope in you.
You are our protector and our shield.

THE PEACE

Pray for peace, look for peace,
speak of peace, act in peace;
accept God's peace.
The peace of the Lord be always with you
and also with you.

THE BLESSING

Know the Mighty God as your strength and your shield: he is
your fortress and your might.
The Lord protect you from all evil and keep you in his love and
peace.
And the blessing...

The Third Sunday of Lent

Isaiah 55. 1–9 : Ps. 63. 1–8 : 1 Corinthians 10. 1–13 : Luke 13. 1–9

Almighty and ever-loving God,
you are more ready to hear us and forgive us than we are to
     come to you.
Forgive us for the times we have sinned and failed you;
strengthen us as we seek to serve you,
that we may follow you in the ways of peace and love;
through Jesus Christ our Lord,
who is alive and reigns with you and the Holy Spirit,
one God, now and for ever. **Amen.**

Lord, we look for you, we long for you, our whole being thirsts
     for you and your love.
Lord, open our eyes, awaken us to what is around us and make
     us aware of your coming.
We pray for all who tend and nurture the young in the faith, for
     all who are growing in awareness of you and your world.
May the church be an instrument of justice and peace in our
     community.
Lord, in your love and mercy,
hear us and help us.

Lord, as you have given us this world to live in, help us to use its
     riches and resources with sensitivity.
Bless and guide all who are working on the land.
We pray for all who supply our food and our daily needs, all
     who are involved in research with crops and cultivation.

Lord, in your love and mercy,
hear us and help us.

We give thanks for our homes and our loved ones.
We pray for our places of work.
May we be faithful and honest in our dealings:
make us sensitive to each other's needs and hopes.
We pray especially for homes with young children.
Lord, in your love and mercy,
hear us and help us.

Lord of love and salvation,
we pray to you for all who are facing disaster in the failure of
   their crops, all suffering because of storms or war, all who
   are victims of violence.
We pray for all who have been taken ill this day or been
   involved in accidents.
We remember friends and loved ones who are ill,
   especially ....
Lord, in your love and mercy,
hear us and help us.

Lord, you are our helper and you protect us from all evil.
We pray for all who will face death today; for our loved ones
   departed, that you will bring them into the fullness of joy in
   your kingdom.
Lord, in your love and mercy,
hear us and help us.

THE PEACE

Christ, the mighty Son of God, deliver you from all evil and fill
you with his peace.
The peace of the Lord be always with you
and also with you.

51

THE BLESSING

The Almighty keep you and protect you from all evil.
The Christ of the cross deliver you from darkness.
The Holy Spirit, guide you in all goodness.
And the blessing...

The Fourth Sunday of Lent

Joshua 5. 9–12 : Ps. 32 : 2 Corinthians 5. 16–21 : Luke 15. 1–3, 11b–32

Lord of all compassion, we return to you like children who had
     wandered away:
we trust in your love, we rejoice in your mercy, we know you
     will accept us.
Lord, enfold us in your peace, and forgive us our sins;
through Jesus Christ your Son our Lord, to whom with you and
     the Holy Spirit be all honour and glory now and for ever.
Amen.

Holy God, when we wander from the way, call us back;
when we stray from the truth, redirect us;
when we do not live life to the full, inspire and refresh us.
May we and your whole church follow him who is the way, the
     truth and the life.
We pray for all who have wandered away from the faith, for all
     who have lost touch with you and your love.
We remember all who are pilgrims and seekers.

Lord, we turn to you.
Enfold us in your peace.

Lord God, we pray for all who have been separated from loved
ones, through war or circumstance, for those who have left
home and become lost.
We remember those who live on the streets of our cities.
We pray for all who live in poverty and debt.
Lord, we turn to you.
Enfold us in your peace.

We give thanks for our families, our parents and all who love
us.
We pray especially for those who are dear to us but with whom
we have lost contact.
We ask your blessing upon all who are taken into care,
for all separated from loved ones through illness.
Lord, we turn to you.
Enfold us in your peace.

Lord, we pray for places where your glory is marred or scarred:
for all who live in slum dwellings,
for all who do not have enough to eat or someone to care for
them.
We remember all lonely and distressed people.
We ask your blessing upon all who are ill at home or in
hospital.
Lord, we turn to you.
Enfold us in your peace.

We pray for all whom you have called home into your kingdom
where sorrow and pain are no more.
We remember especially ....
Lord, we turn to you.
Enfold us in your peace.

The God of love forgives you, accepts you and enfolds you in
his peace.
The peace of the Lord be always with you
and also with you.

The Father comes to meet you in love.
The Son comes to you with forgiveness.
The Spirit comes to refresh and restore you.
And the blessing...

The Fifth Sunday of Lent
(Passiontide begins)

Isaiah 43. 16–21 : Ps. 126 : Philippians 3. 4b–14 : John 12. 1–8

Almighty God, we give you thanks for your great love towards
us and the whole world, love revealed in our Lord Jesus Christ,
who by his death destroyed death, and who has for us opened
the gate of glory. We pray that, sharing in the fellowship of the
suffering of our Lord, we may come to know the power of his
resurrection; through the same Christ our Lord, who is alive
and reigns with you and the Holy Spirit, one God, now and for
ever. **Amen.**

We give thanks for all who are contemplatives:
for those who teach others to meditate,
for all who have shown us how to be silent before you.
Lord, in the stillness of this place, refresh us;
in the stillness of our minds, renew us;
in the quiet of our hearts, restore us.
We pray for all who are caught up in hyperactivity,
all who seek to justify themselves by work, all who cannot be
    still.
Lord, we come before you.
Change us and we shall be changed.

We give thanks for those who work to provide for us.
We pray for all who grow produce and prepare our food,
for all who cater and all who provide hospitality for others,
for all who work in shops and supermarkets.
Lord, we come before you.
Change us and we shall be changed.

Lord, we are grateful for places of rest and peace:
we thank you for our homes and all who care for us.
We pray for all who are overworked in their caring for others.
We ask your blessing on all who have shared their time and
    their love with us.
Lord, we come before you.
Change us and we shall be changed.

Lord, we pray that through your cross and passion we may
    come to know the power of your resurrection.
We remember before you all suffering peoples, all who are
    struggling or despairing at this time,
all who are facing darkness or death.
May they come to rejoice in your presence and saving power.
Lord, we come before you.
Change us and we shall be changed.

We give thanks for all who have passed through pain and
    suffering and are now where sorrow and pain are no more,
for all who have experienced the power of your resurrection.
We pray especially for ....
Lord, we come before you.
Change us and we shall be changed.

THE PEACE

They that wait upon the Lord shall renew their strength.
The peace of the Lord be always with you
and also with you.

THE BLESSING

Abide in the love of the Father who upholds you.
Abide in the peace of the Son who enfolds you.
Abide in the power of the Spirit who sustains you.
And the blessing ...

Palm Sunday (Liturgy of the Passion)

Isaiah 50. 4–9a : Ps. 31. 9–16 [17–18] : Philippians 2. 5–11 : Luke 22.14 – 23.56 *or*
Luke 23. 1–49

God, our Father, as Christ was welcomed into the Holy City,
may we welcome him into our lives and homes. May the King
of Glory have rule in our hearts, that your kingdom come in us

as it is in heaven; through Christ our Lord, to whom with you, Father, and the Holy Spirit be all praise, honour and glory for ever and ever. **Amen.**

Holy God, teach us humility, that we may not lord it over
  anyone, that we may be gentle and gracious in our dealings.
We pray that your church may work for the coming of your
  kingdom, by seeking to do your will and to work for your
  glory.
We remember Christians working in deprived areas, and in
  areas where they are persecuted because of their faith.
Christ, by your passion,
protect us.

We pray for communities that are oppressed, for areas where
  community living is breaking down.
We pray for fractured and fragmented peoples, remembering
  the refugees and war-torn peoples of our world.
We pray for all who risk their lives in caring for others.
Christ, by your passion,
protect us.

We give thanks for all who have protected us,
for loved ones who have seen to our growth and well-being.
Bless all who have lost their homes and possessions this week;
we remember especially children taken into care and children
  whose lives are in danger.
Christ, by your passion,
protect us.

We bring before you the troubles of people and nations, praying
  especially for ....
Lord, by your suffering, save us;
by your hurt, heal us;
by your death, deliver us;
by your resurrection, raise us up.

Christ, by your passion,
protect us.

King of kings, we pray for all who have entered into the joy of
    your kingdom,
all who have found new peace and life in you.
Christ, by your passion,
protect us.

THE PEACE

The King of Glory, the Prince of Peace comes to you. Hosanna
(Praise God).
The peace of the Lord be always with you
and also with you.

THE BLESSING

In the passion of the Lord is your protection,
in his suffering is your salvation,
in his hurt is your healing,
in his death is your deliverance;
and the blessing . . .

Easter

Easter Day

Acts 10. 34–43 *or* Isaiah 65. 17–25 : Ps. 118 [1–2] 14–24 : 1 Corinthians 15. 19–26 *or* Acts 10. 34–43 : John 20. 1–18 *or* Luke 24. 1–12

Alleluia to our God, who has given us the victory.
Alleluia to our God, who has broken the power of death.
Alleluia to our God, who has defeated the depths of darkness.
Alleluia to our God, who has triumphed over evil.
Alleluia to our God, who has won for us life eternal.
In love we give ourselves to you, holy Lord.
In joy we worship you, mighty Son of the Father.
In you is our hope, O Christ, who died and now is risen, and
    lives with the Father and the Holy Spirit, one God, for ever
    and ever. **Amen.**

Let the whole church rejoice, in city and in open country,
in this land and throughout the world, for Christ is risen.
Let each congregation and fellowship rejoice,
let each heart and mind rejoice, for Christ is risen.
O Lord, may we and the whole church rejoice in your victory,
let us proclaim the Good News that death is defeated;
we are set free and Christ has won for us the victory.
May we reflect your glory and the power of your resurrection.

Lord, may we know you
and the power of your resurrection.

We pray for all who are struggling for peace,
all who are longing for new hope and new life.
We remember war-torn cities and places that have suffered
from disasters;
we pray for all who are seeking to rebuild communities and
lives,
all who are bringing new life and courage to oppressed peoples.
Lord, may we know you
and the power of your resurrection.

Let the power of the resurrection be known in our homes:
in you, risen Lord, may relationships be strengthened and
restored;
in you, risen Lord, may hurts be healed and well-being restored.
We pray for homes where there is violence or neglect.
Lord, may we know you
and the power of your resurrection.

We pray for all struggling peoples, that they may find hope in
you.
We pray for the chronically ill, for all who walk in darkness,
for all who are in pain, and all who have lost hope,
for all distressed or disturbed peoples,
for those who are terminally ill and those near to death.
Lord, may we know you
and the power of your resurrection.

We remember all who have lost loved ones, who are deeply
bereaved and in great sorrow.
We pray for loved ones departed,
    especially ....
May we seek to know they rejoice where sorrow and pain are
no more.

Lord, may we know you
and the power of your resurrection.

THE PEACE

The Prince of Peace has conquered death and given us the victory.
In him we are more than conquerors.
The peace of the Lord be always with you, alleluia,
and also with you, alleluia.

THE BLESSING

May you know in your life the presence of the risen Lord, the peace of Christ who is the eternal, and the power of his resurrection; and the blessing...

The Second Sunday of Easter

Acts 5. 27–32 : Ps. 118. 14–29 *or* Ps. 150 : Revelation 1. 4–8 : John 20. 19–31

Christ our Lord, risen from the dead,
come and enter into the darkness of our doubt and despair,
     with the bright light of your presence,
that we may put our trust in you and in the power of your
     resurrection,
that we may rejoice in you the risen Lord, our Saviour,
who lives and reigns with the Father and the Holy Spirit,
one God, world without end. **Amen.**

Lord our God, we pray that we may see you through faith:
in seeing you, we will begin to know you;
in knowing you, we will give ourselves in love to you;
and in loving you, we will enjoy your presence for ever.
We thank you for all who have shared their vision and insights,
for all who have shared their awareness and love for you.
We pray for all who seek to proclaim the Good News of the
gospel.
May all who are involved in ministry reveal your love and your
saving power.
We remember all who are new to the faith, and the newly
baptized,
for all who are seekers and those who do not know of your
love.
Jesus, come among us
in your risen power.

We pray for leaders of nations and governments, for all in
authority,
that they may be wise and gentle in their dealings,
that they may be caring and respectful of others.
We pray for those seeking to rescue the poor and any who are in
danger.
We pray for the emergency services and all who risk their lives
for others.
Jesus, come among us
in your risen power.

We ask that we may come to know your presence and power in
our lives, in our homes, and in our neighbours.
We pray for homes where there is strain and stress at this time,
for families who have lost a loved one, or who have been
betrayed in love;
that we may all know of your love and care for us.
Jesus, come among us
in your risen power.

We remember all who have had a hard week this week and all
who look in fear towards the future.
We pray for those who have been awake all night and are weary
and worn,
for the over-anxious, the depressed and the dispirited,
for those who have watched over the ill and the suffering.
We remember friends and loved ones with special needs and
hopes.
Jesus, come among us
in your risen power.

Lord, grant grace and peace to the departed:
may they rejoice in the fullness of life eternal.
Lord, grant that we may put our trust in you now and in the
hour of our death.
Jesus, come among us
in your risen power.

THE PEACE

The presence and power of the risen Lord fill you with all joy
and peace.
The peace of the Lord be always with you
and also with you.

THE BLESSING

The power and peace of the risen Lord be with you to protect
you.
The grace and goodness of the Lord of life go with you,
that you may dwell in him and he in you;
and the blessing . . .

The Third Sunday of Easter

Acts 9. 1–6 [7–20] : Ps. 30 : Revelation 5. 11–14 : John 21. 1–19

Lord, you came down to lift us up,
you became human that we might share in the divine,
you died that we might rise to life immortal.
Help us to live as those who believe and trust in you,
and grant that we may live to your praise and glory,
Christ our Lord, who rose for us and now lives and reigns with
   the Father and the Holy Spirit, one God, now and for ever.
   Amen.

Lord, you are the Lord of life, in your presence is the fullness of
   joy.
We pray to you for all whose vocations have been frustrated by
   illness, oppression, opposition or circumstance:
may they not lose hope, and discover that in every situation you
   are there and call them.
We pray for those who preach your word in areas where there is
   little or no response,
all who witness to you among opposition and violence.
We pray for all who celebrate the Holy Communion and who
   minister the sacraments.
God of hope,
fill us with joy and peace in believing.

We give thanks for lively and vital communities.
We pray for the individuals that help to restore and hold
   together community life.

We pray for people in areas where community has broken
down,
for down-town areas of fear and poverty,
for those who have left home with nowhere to go.
We remember all who sleep rough and the organizations that
care for them.
God of hope,
fill us with joy and peace in believing.

We give thanks for those who share their lives with us,
our families, our friends and our neighbours.
We pray for any who are finding life difficult or distressing,
for those whose relationships are breaking down,
for homes where there is sorrow and darkness.
God of hope,
fill us with joy and peace in believing.

Lord, bless all who work hard for little or no reward,
all who find no rest from their toil or their fear.
We pray for all whose lives are full of guilt, regret and remorse,
for those who have lost faith in themselves or in the world
around them.
We pray for all who have been involved in accidents or acts of
violence.
We remember friends and loved ones who are ill.
God of hope,
fill us with joy and peace in believing.

Lord, we give thanks that you will seek us out and bring us
safely home.
We pray for those you have enfolded in the love and peace of
your kingdom.
We pray especially for ....
We pray that you will keep them in life and joy everlasting.
God of hope,
fill us with joy and peace in believing.

THE PEACE

The Lord seeks out and saves the lost,
he restores the fallen and rescues the perishing.
The peace of the Lord be always with you
and also with you.

THE BLESSING

The Mighty God, who brought again from the dead our Lord
Jesus Christ, take you into his protection, enfold you with his
love, direct you on your journey; and the blessing...

The Fourth Sunday of Easter

Acts 9. 36–43 : Ps. 23 : Revelation 7. 9–17 : John 10. 22–30

Good and gracious God, be our shepherd and our guide:
lead us out of darkness and death and into life and light eternal;
deliver us from all evil, guide us into the ways of goodness and
   peace,
and when we wander bring us back to you and your love;
through Jesus Christ our Lord,
who is alive and reigns with you, O Father, and the Holy Spirit,
one God, for ever and ever. **Amen.**

Good Shepherd, we ask you to be our guide:
lead us out of darkness,
lead us out of trouble,
lead us out of fear,

lead us out of death,
and bring us to the fullness of life eternal.
We rejoice with the saints and the whole company of heaven
and say, 'Salvation belongs to our God'.
We pray for all pastors and those who have the care of your
people;
we remember those who are spiritual directors and counsellors.
Faithful Shepherd, lead us from darkness to light,
from death to life eternal.

We pray for all who direct the minds of the young, for teachers,
and for all who broadcast through radio and television.
We give thanks and pray for those who provide us with food
through farming and agriculture, for those who provide for
us in shops and supermarkets.
Faithful Shepherd, lead us from darkness to light,
from death to life eternal.

We remember before you all who have been our teachers and
guides;
we pray for our local schools and places of learning.
We ask your blessing upon our communities, our homes and
our loved ones.
We pray for all who have lost direction, for all who have lost
faith in themselves, in the world and in their God.
We pray for the despondent, the disillusioned and the
despairing, for all who feel desperate or distressed,
that they may know that God seeks for them and loves them.
We pray for all who are ill or struggling at this time,
especially ....
Faithful Shepherd, lead us from darkness to light,
from death to life eternal.

We rejoice that you lead us through the valley of the shadow of
death and offer us life eternal.
We pray for all who rejoice in your love and in your kingdom.
We pray especially for ....

Faithful Shepherd, lead us from darkness to light,
from death to life eternal.

THE PEACE

Jesus is the Good Shepherd and leads us into the way of peace.
The peace of the Lord be always with you
and also with you.

THE BLESSING

The faithful Shepherd protect you from all evil,
strengthen you with his goodness,
lead you to the fullness of his love;
and the blessing . . .

The Fifth Sunday of Easter

Acts 11. 1–18 : Ps. 148. 1–6 [7–14] : Revelation 21. 1–6 : John 13. 31–35

Lord Jesus Christ, Son of the Father,
give us wisdom and faith to trust in you.
When we cannot see your presence,
when the way is full of darkness and doubt,
increase our faith and help us to know that you will never leave
   us or forsake us,
for you are ever with us, Jesus Christ our Lord,
to whom with the Father and the Holy Spirit
be all honour and glory, now and for ever. **Amen.**

Lord, we rejoice that we abide in you and in your great love;
you accept us when we find it hard to accept ourselves or each
other.
We pray that you will strengthen the fellowship of your people,
that you will sustain us in our unity and help us to know we are
one in you.
We pray for all who are striving to realize the unity that you
give to your church.
We pray for inter-church relationships and all groups that help
to break down barriers.
Lord, lead us from despair to hope,
from division to wholeness.

Lord, we remember before you all areas of ethnic violence and
racial hatred,
for all places where there is division, strife and animosity.
We pray for the United Nations and for all who work for peace
and unity,
for all peoples that work for the building up of community and
fellowship.
We remember all who are scorned, rejected or belittled by
others.
Lord, lead us from despair to hope,
from division to wholeness.

We give thanks for our own homes and their love.
We pray for homes of strife and discord, homes where there is
neglect, abuse or violence.
We remember homes where there is no love or where love is
betrayed.
We pray for all families suffering from a breakdown in their
relationships.
Lord, lead us from despair to hope,
from division to wholeness.

We pray for all who suffer from schizophrenia,
for those whose lives are torn apart by memories or fears.

We pray for all who have suffered from any form of
  breakdown.
We ask your blessing on loved ones and friends who are
  suffering at this time:
we pray especially for ....
Lord, lead us from despair to hope,
from division to wholeness.

We look forward to the day when we will share fully in the
  communion of saints, when we will be one in the Spirit and
  one in the Lord.
We pray for loved ones departed, for all who have gone before
  us in the faith, and for the day when we will share with them
  in your kingdom.
Lord, lead us from despair to hope,
from division to wholeness.

THE PEACE

The risen Lord gives new strength to his people and offers them
life and peace.
The peace of the Lord be always with you
and also with you.

THE BLESSING

The joy of the resurrection be yours.
The power of the risen Lord protect you.
The peace of the Lord of life give you wholeness.
And the blessing...

The Sixth Sunday of Easter

Acts 16. 9–15 : Ps. 67 : Revelation 21.10, 22 – 22.5 : John 14. 23–29 *or* John 5. 1–9

Lord Jesus Christ, who promised that in you we would find
    peace,
give us that peace which the world cannot give,
the deep peace of God which passes all understanding.
In all our troubles and anxieties, keep us calm and hopeful;
grant that we may know we abide in you and in your peace;
through Jesus Christ our Lord,
who lives and reigns with the Father and the Holy Spirit,
one God, now and for ever. **Amen.**

Lord, we put our trust in you, and in you is our rest.
We pray for all pilgrim peoples as they journey through this
    world, for all seekers, for those who search for truth and
    integrity.
May we and your whole church live as those travelling into
    your love and deeper into your presence.
We pray today for places of pilgrimage, and places of special
    holiness, for all who act as guides to others on their
    pilgrimage.
God, as you call us to you,
guide us in our journey.

We remember before you all who are homeless, all who have
    been made refugees by war and oppression.
We pray for those who live rough and who sleep out in our
    cities.

71

We pray for travelling peoples and gypsies.
God, as you call us to you,
guide us in our journey.

We give thanks for our homes and places of security, where we
    find love, rest and refreshment.
May your Spirit be at home in our homes,
may your ways be known to us and may we walk in them.
We pray for guidance in our journey through life,
for ourselves, our families and our loved ones.
God, as you call us to you,
guide us in our journey.

Lord of peace, give rest to the weary, the worn and the fearful;
give peace to the anxious, the troubled and the distressed.
We pray for all who have lost courage or hope in their journey,
all whose way seems dark and threatening.
We pray for the troubled in body, mind or spirit,
for all who are ill,
    especially ....
God, as you call us to you,
guide us in our journey.

We give thanks for all who have come to their journey's end on
    earth:
may they find rest and peace and life in you.
We pray for the day when we will be one with them in your
    eternal kingdom.
God, as you call us to you,
guide us in our journey.

THE PEACE

Christ our Saviour comes to each of us and gives us that peace
which the world cannot give.

The peace of the Lord be always with you
and also with you.

THE BLESSING

The goodness of the Father go with you.
The love of the Saviour lead you.
The grace of the Spirit guide you.
And the blessing . . .

Ascension Day

Acts 1. 1–11 *or* Daniel 7. 9–14 : Ps. 47 *or* Ps. 93 : Ephesians 1. 15–23 *or*
Acts 1. 1–11 : Luke 24. 44–53

Glory to you, Christ our King, you came down to lift us up,
you became human that we might share in the divine.
Lift our hearts and minds that we may behold your glory
and proclaim you as our Saviour and King,
who lives and reigns with the Father and the Holy Spirit,
one God, now and for ever. **Amen.**

Lord unseen, yet ever near, your presence may we feel.
We pray for all whose lives are clouded by deep doubt and fear,
for all who have lost faith, for all whose vision has become
blurred.
We pray that the church may proclaim and reveal your presence
and glory,
that the church may help to lift up the fallen and restore sight to
the blind.

73

We pray for those with strong vision and faith, that they may
    guide us to you.
Christ, King of Glory,
lift our hearts and minds.

We pray for all who have been separated from loved ones by
    war, illness or circumstance.
For those who are searching for loved ones, for all who feel
    lonely and deserted.
We remember those whose lives are clouded by tyranny and
    oppression,
all who are anxious about their future and their loved ones.
Christ, King of Glory,
lift our hearts and minds.

We give thanks that you are with us always.
May we be at home with you in our homes;
let our dwellings reflect your glory and love.
We pray for our families and neighbours,
for all our friends, especially those we seldom see.
Christ, King of Glory,
lift our hearts and minds.

We remember all who feel broken-hearted or dis-spirited,
all who are down and need someone to uplift them.
We pray for all who are chronically ill and all who care for the
    terminally ill.
We remember friends and loved ones in their troubles.
Christ, King of Glory,
lift our hearts and minds.

We rejoice that you have ascended into glory and have opened
    the kingdom of heaven to all believers.
As you came to lift us out of darkness into eternal light,
and out of death into life eternal,
we pray for all who are bereaved and mourn.
We pray for loved ones whom you have lifted up into your
    kingdom.

Christ, King of Glory,
lift our hearts and minds.

THE PEACE

Christ, the risen and ascended Lord, comes to lift us into his
kingdom of light and peace.
The peace of the Lord be always with you
and also with you.

THE BLESSING

Christ, the ascended Lord, be with you always,
to uplift you out of darkness and death,
to inspire, guide and give you a glimpse of his glory;
and the blessing...

The Seventh Sunday of Easter
(Sunday after Ascension Day)

Acts 16. 16–34 : Ps. 97 : Revelation 22. 12–14, 16–17, 20–21 : John 17. 20–26

Almighty Father, who through your great love raised your Son
into glory, help us to know we are not alone, to know we dwell
in you and you in us, to know that the ascended Lord is with us
always, and that your Spirit comes to guide and strengthen us.
Lord, as we come before you, grant us a glimpse of your glory;

we ask this in the name of our Lord Jesus Christ, who with you
and the Holy Spirit are one God, now and for ever. **Amen.**

Mighty God, as we come before your glory,
fill us with your Spirit,
renew our vision,
restore our faith,
refresh your church.
Lord, we pray that the whole church may wait upon you and
show the gifts of the Spirit.
We pray especially for ministers and peoples who are losing
vision, for all who have lost faith, and are without hope.
Lord of glory, change us
and we shall be changed.

We pray for the leaders of the nations,
that they may serve with integrity and justice,
that they may be aware that their gifts and power come from
you.
We pray for world unity and peace, for the time when the
kingdoms of the world will become the kingdom of Christ
our Lord.
Lord of glory, change us
and we shall be changed.

Lord, grant that in our homes we may learn to wait upon you,
make us sensitive to each other and our needs;
as you give us gifts, may we freely share them with others.
Lord, teach us all to be gracious and generous.
Lord of glory, change us
and we shall be changed.

Lord, may the glory of your presence transform lives that are
dull and drab.
We pray that all dis-spirited people may discover your Spirit in
their lives.
We bring before you all who are down and distressed,

all who are weak and discouraged, for your uplifting, O God.
We pray for friends and loved ones who are struggling at this
time, who are ill or weary.
Lord of glory, change us
and we shall be changed.

We give thanks that when we face death we have hope;
you renew us by your spirit and restore us in your love.
We pray for all who have passed through death and rejoice in
life eternal.
Lord of glory, change us
and we shall be changed.

THE PEACE

The Lord is King, let the earth rejoice, let the multitude of the
islands be glad, for he comes in peace to renew his people.
The peace of the Lord be always with you
and also with you.

THE BLESSING

Rejoice in the Lord, give thanks to his holy Name, for he
restores and renews his people; and the blessing ...

Day of Pentecost

Acts 2. 1–21 or Genesis 11. 1–9 : Ps. 104. 24–34, 35b (or 24–36) :
Romans 8. 14–17 or Acts 2. 1–21 : John 14. 8–17 [25–27]

Holy Father, fill us with the Holy Spirit, the power of the living
  God.
Guide us by the Holy Spirit, the giver of light and life.
Strengthen us through the Holy Spirit, the fire of love.
Let your Spirit come upon us and change us and all your
  faithful people,
that we may live and work to your praise and glory;
through Jesus Christ our Lord,
who is alive and reigns with you and the Holy Spirit,
one God, now and for ever. **Amen.**

Holy God, we give thanks for the coming of the Spirit to your
  church.
We ask that the gifts of the Spirit may be revealed in all your
  people:
may the church share the gifts that you have given to it;
may we go out in the power of the Spirit to proclaim your love
  and your glory.
We praise you and pray for all who have the gifts of ministry,
  preaching and pastoral care, for gifted musicians and singers,
  for hymn-writers and leaders of worship.
We pray that through the Spirit our worship may be lively and
  relevant.
Breathe on us, Breath of God,
and fill us with life anew.

We pray for all who through their talents enrich and beautify
    our world, for artists, writers, craftspeople and broadcasters,
for all who communicate and all who work in education,
for all those who through their talents provide us with food and
    clothing.
We remember all whose talent is unused through fear or
    opposition,
all who feel thwarted in their ambitions and talents.
Breathe on us, Breath of God,
and fill us with life anew.

We give you thanks for the working of the Spirit in our lives,
for the gifts we have and the guidance we have received.
We pray for those who have been our teachers and educators,
for all who have brought us into a fuller and richer life.
We remember our homes and our loved ones.
Breathe on us, Breath of God,
and fill us with life anew.

We pray for all who feel fearful and close themselves in,
for those who are locked in by anxiety or guilt,
for all who are afraid to venture and risk.
We remember all whose lives are restricted by illness or
    disability,
all who are frustrated by being limited by circumstances.
We pray for loved ones who are ill,
    especially ....
Breathe on us, Breath of God,
and fill us with life anew.

We give thanks that you are the God who breathes new life
    into us;
you are the God who restores and refreshes us.
We give thanks that you give us new life in your kingdom.
We remember before you our friends and loved ones departed
and pray that they may share with your saints in glory.

Breathe on us, Breath of God,
and fill us with life anew.

THE PEACE

The Spirit of the Lord comes upon us to renew us and the face
of the whole earth, and to bring us into his peace.
The peace of the Lord be always with you
and also with you.

THE BLESSING

The Spirit of the living God,
give fire to your faith,
breathe new life into worship,
give new power to your witness;
and the blessing . . .

Ordinary Time

Trinity Sunday

Proverbs 8. 1–4, 22–31 : Ps. 8 : Romans 5. 1–5 : John 16. 12–15

Father, in love you created us.
Christ, by love you redeemed us.
Spirit, through love you sustain us.
We pray that by the power of your love, that binds you as Three
and One, we may give ourselves in joy and love to you,
Father, Son and Holy Spirit. **Amen.**

Father, we give you thanks for creation, for the beauty, wonder
and order of our universe.
We give thanks that we are fearfully and wonderfully made.
We pray for the work of your church in conservation and
preservation,
that we may reflect your love for the world.
We pray that the church may give strength to family life and
society.
Holy, holy, holy God,
hear us and have mercy.

Lord and Saviour, Jesus Christ, we give thanks for your love in
redemption.
We pray for the emergency services and for relief agencies, for
all who risk their lives and give their lives for others.

We pray for all who are seeking to bring healing and peace to our world, all who are working for unity and harmony.
Holy, holy, holy God,
hear us and have mercy.

Holy Spirit of God, we give thanks for the life you breathe into us, for the talents and abilities you give to us.
We give you thanks and pray for our homes, our communities and our places of work.
We ask that you will guide us into ways of justice and peace.
We pray for teachers of the faith, preachers and theologians.
Holy, holy, holy God,
hear us and have mercy.

We pray for all who do not know or love you, O God,
for all who have not become aware of your mystery and wonder,
for all who do not feel or trust in your presence.
We remember doubters and those who despair,
all who suffer through illness, neglect or violence.
We remember, in your presence, friends and loved ones in need, sickness or any other adversity.
Holy, holy, holy God,
hear us and have mercy.

We give thanks for the mystery of the Trinity and seek to enjoy the wonder of Three Persons in One God.
We rejoice that you are our Creator, Redeemer and Sustainer, and, as you have made us, you give us life eternal.
We pray for all who have come closer to your threefold presence and enjoy your fellowship.
We pray especially for ....
Holy, holy, holy God,
hear us and have mercy.

God the Creator provides you with his peace.
Christ the Redeemer gives you his peace.
The Holy Spirit fills you with his peace.
The peace of the Lord be always with you
and also with you.

THE BLESSING

The Father of all enfold you in his love.
Christ the Saviour keep you in life eternal.
The Holy Spirit fill you with his grace.
And the blessing...

Proper 4

Sunday between 29 May and 4 June inclusive (if after Trinity Sunday)

———

Track 1	*Track 2*
1 Kings 18. 20–21 [22–29] 30–39	1 Kings 8. 22–23, 41–43
Ps. 96	Ps. 96. 1–9
Galatians 1. 1–12	Galatians 1. 1–12
Luke 7. 1–10	Luke 7. 1–10

Lord of majesty and splendour, the King of all creation, from
you comes all wholeness, peace and well-being. We come with
our needs and in our brokenness, seeking your help and
knowing that you alone can make us whole. Come, Lord, and
renew us; through Jesus Christ our Lord, who is alive and

reigns with you and the Holy Spirit, one God, now and for ever. **Amen.**

Holy and ever-loving God, we come before you in love and adoration:
you only are the Lord, you alone are God most high.
We pray for all who have lost their faith, for all who have ceased to worship you, for all who have been led away to chase after things that are not God.
We pray for your whole church and its faithfulness to you:
all who witness to your presence,
all who declare your love,
all who reveal your glory in their lives,
all who go out in mission.
We pray that they may remain strong in their faith.
O Lord Almighty and ever with us,
hear us and help us.

We pray for all who have the care of others, for all the caring professions.
We pray for teachers, doctors, nurses and medical workers,
for all who have the care of children and young people,
for all who support the elderly and the infirm.
O Lord Almighty and ever with us,
hear us and help us.

We give you thanks for all who have been a support and help to us.
We pray for those who have been our guides and protectors,
for those who inspire us and those who love us;
we remember all who have shared their lives and their love with us, especially ....
O Lord Almighty and ever with us,
hear us and help us.

We bring before you all who suffer from loneliness or neglect:
we pray for any who lack love or support in their lives.

We remember today all whose minds have lost their reason;
we pray for all who have become difficult to live with, and for
their loved ones;
we think of all who live in confusion or deep despair.
We pray for friends and loved ones who are ill,
especially ....
O Lord Almighty and ever with us,
hear us and help us.

We give thanks for all who have entered the fuller presence of
God.
We give thanks for the saints and all the holy ones of God.
We pray for our loved ones who are departed this life.
O Lord Almighty and ever with us,
hear us and help us.

THE PEACE

Grace and peace be to you from our mighty God, from Father,
Son and Holy Spirit.
The peace of the Lord be always with you
and also with you.

THE BLESSING

The strength of God be your support.
The light of God be your guide.
The love of God be your joy.
And the blessing . . .

Proper 5

Sunday between 5 and 11 June inclusive (if after Trinity Sunday)

Track 1
1 Kings 17. 8–16 [17–24]
Ps. 146
Galatians 1. 11–24
Luke 7. 11–17

Track 2
1 Kings 17. 17–24
Ps. 30
Galatians 1. 11–24
Luke 7. 11–17

Lord of our life and God of our salvation, we cry out to you;
we come to you for hope and for healing,
we come for health and for wholeness.
Come, Lord, and touch us and renew us;
through Jesus Christ our Lord, who is alive and reigns with
  you, O Father, and the Holy Spirit, now and for ever. **Amen.**

Lord, strengthen our faith in the resurrection,
increase our hope in eternal life,
give us courage and a deep trust in you.
We pray for all who seek to support others in their faith,
for all preachers of the word and ministers of the sacraments,
for all who are pastoral visitors, for counsellors and spiritual
  directors.
Lord, we put our trust in you
and in your saving power.

We remember all who are oppressed, hungry and homeless,
all who are in danger of losing hope and their dignity.
We pray for leaders of peoples, that they may be
  compassionate, caring and supportive.

We pray for all who deal with world poverty and world debt.
Lord, we put our trust in you
and in your saving power.

Lord, grant us sensitivity in our dealings with others;
make us aware of the needs of those around us;
keep us generous and gracious in all our dealings.
We pray for our homes and our places of work, for our friends
and our loved ones.
Lord, we put our trust in you
and in your saving power.

We remember before you all who have suffered a bereavement,
those who have lost a parent, all orphaned children,
for all who are suffering due to loss of a loved one.
We pray for the lonely, the sad, all who long for love and
acceptance.
We pray for all who have been separated from their loved ones
through illness.
We remember especially ....
Lord, we put our trust in you
and in your saving power.

God of compassion and love, we give thanks for all who have
awoken to joy in the morning of eternity.
We pray for all who have passed through pain and death and
rejoice in your presence in newness of life,
especially ....
Lord, we put our trust in you
and in your saving power.

THE PEACE

The Lord who is our light and salvation gives us himself and his
peace.
The peace of the Lord be always with you
and also with you.

The God of hope, give you courage in your troubles.
Christ the Redeemer give you the joy of salvation.
The Holy Spirit of God be your strength in times of weakness.
And the blessing...

Proper 6

Sunday between 12 and 18 June inclusive (if after Trinity Sunday)

———

Track 1
1 Kings 21. 1–10 [11–14] 15–21a
Ps. 5. 1–8
Galatians 2. 15–21
Luke 7.36 – 8.3

Track 2
2 Samuel 11.26 – 12.10, 13–15
Ps. 32
Galatians 2. 15–21
Luke 7.36 – 8.3

Lord God of love, as you come to us and give yourself for us
and to us, make us aware of your coming and your generosity,
that we may rejoice in your presence and give our love to you;
through Jesus Christ our Lord, who is alive and reigns with you
and the Holy Spirit, one God, now and for ever. **Amen.**

Father, we give thanks for all who have enriched the church by
    their faith.
We pray for those called to be pastors and shepherds of your
    flock, especially any who are being called to offer themselves
    for ordination at this time.
We remember those who teach in Sunday schools and day
    schools, those who preach the word and administer the
    sacraments.

We pray for religious communities and missionary societies, for
soul friends, confessors and spiritual counsellors.
Lord, have mercy.
Forgive us and heal us.

We ask that we may all know your forgiveness.
We pray for all who are in prison,
all who are locked up by guilt and remorse.
We remember all who stand for justice and freedom,
all who show forgiveness and help people to live in harmony.
We pray for communities divided by past violence.
Lord, have mercy.
Forgive us and heal us.

We give thanks for all who have been forgiving towards us,
all who have taught us about forgiveness and love.
We pray for our loved ones and friends.
We pray for relationships that are marred by past sins and
errors,
for all who are unable to forgive and start afresh.
Lord, have mercy.
Forgive us and heal us.

We pray for all who are being destroyed by guilt,
all who are unable to accept forgiveness and be changed.
We ask for your blessing upon all who are troubled by
memories of the past.
We remember before you friends and loved ones who are ill.
We pray especially for all who feel betrayed or deserted by
others.
Lord, have mercy.
Forgive us and heal us.

We give thanks for the forgiveness of sins and the resurrection
of the body.
We pray for all our friends who are departed this life,
that they may be numbered with your saints in glory
everlasting.

Lord, have mercy.
Forgive us and heal us.

THE PEACE

The Father offers you life and peace.
The Son offers you salvation and forgiveness.
The Spirit offers you restoration and renewal.
The peace of the Lord be always with you
and also with you.

THE BLESSING

God, our Father and Creator, gives you his love.
Christ, our Saviour, gives you salvation from your sins.
The Holy Spirit of God gives you newness of life.
And the blessing . . .

Proper 7

Sunday between 19 and 25 June inclusive (if after Trinity Sunday)

———

Track 1
1 Kings 19. 1–4 [5–7] 8–15a
Ps. 42; 43 (*or* 42 *or* 43)
Galatians 3. 23–29
Luke 8. 26–39

Track 2
Isaiah 65. 1–9
Ps. 22. 19–28
Galatians 3. 23–29
Luke 8. 26–39

Lord of light and truth, who in Jesus gives peace to our hearts
and minds and renews and refreshes our whole being, may we

know that you are an ever-present help in trouble. Lord, heal us
and we shall be healed, strengthen us to work for you; through
Jesus Christ our Saviour and Redeemer, who lives and reigns
with you and the Holy Spirit, one God, now and for ever.
Amen.

God of love and compassion,
you are always more ready to hear and help than we are to
    pray;
help us to know that you are with us now and always and that
    you are a very present help in trouble.
We pray for all who come to your church with hopes and fears,
all who come with special needs, that in you they may find new
    hope.
We remember all who thirst for God, we pray for pilgrims and
    seekers.
Lord, we wait upon you.
You are our helper and deliverer.

We pray for our troubled world, for places of oppression,
    tyranny and violence.
We remember all who suffer through war or natural disasters.
We ask your blessing upon the hungry and the homeless,
all who have no place to call their own.
Lord, we wait upon you.
You are our helper and deliverer.

We give thanks for all who have shared their love and peace
    with us;
we pray for our homes and our loved ones.
We pray for homes where there is trouble, for destitute families,
for those who have been evicted or driven out of their homes.
We pray for homes where there is abuse or neglect.
Lord, we wait upon you.
You are our helper and deliverer.

We remember before you all who are not at peace with
   themselves or their neighbours,
all who are troubled in body, mind or spirit.
We pray for all who feel despised or rejected,
all who walk in fear and in darkness.
We pray for members of our community who are ill,
   especially ....
Lord, we wait upon you.
You are our helper and deliverer.

We give thanks that you are our strength in times of weakness;
you deliver us from the power of death.
We give thanks for all who have been delivered from eternal
   death, and pray for loved ones departed this life.
Lord, we wait upon you.
You are our helper and deliverer.

THE PEACE

The grace of God is sufficient to meet all our needs,
his power is revealed in our weakness,
in our troubles he gives us his peace.
The peace of the Lord be always with you
and also with you.

THE BLESSING

The hand of God protect you.
The peace of Christ be with you.
The power of the Spirit strengthen you.
And the blessing ...

Proper 8

Sunday between 26 June and 2 July inclusive

Track 1
2 Kings 2. 1–2, 6–14
Ps. 77. [1–2] 11–20
Galatians 5. 1, 13–25
Luke 9. 51–62

Track 2
1 Kings 19. 15–16, 19–21
Ps. 16
Galatians 5. 1, 13–25
Luke 9. 51–62

Spirit of the living God, come fill us,
that we may live in joy and peace,
and that our lives may show the gifts of patience, kindness and
    generosity;
that we may live in faithfulness, gentleness and self-control
    through your power working within us.
We ask this in the name of Jesus Christ, who lives and reigns
    with the Father and you, blessed Spirit, now and for ever.
Amen.

Mighty God, we pray that all people may have freedom to fulfil
    their vocations.
Within your church may each find their ministry and calling.
We pray for the newly baptized, those being confirmed and for
    new converts,
that your church may grow in holiness, in outreach and in
    number.
We ask you to guide and direct all who go out in mission,
all who preach the word and all who administer the sacraments.
Show us the path of life.
Lord, hear us, graciously hear us.

We ask that you will guide all who are called to govern,
all who are in positions of authority or influence.
We pray for the work of the United Nations and its peace-
keeping forces.
We remember all who work in conservation and deal gently
with the earth.
Show us the path of life.
Lord; hear us, graciously hear us.

We give thanks for all who have enriched our lives by their
talents and gifts.
Bless, O Lord, our homes and communities;
make them places of gentleness and generosity,
places of grace and goodness,
places of holiness and hospitality,
and begin now with us.
Show us the path of life.
Lord, hear us, graciously hear us.

We remember before you all who are restricted by poverty or
oppression,
all who cannot fulfil their calling due to illness or circumstance.
We pray for all who are afraid to commit themselves to anyone.
We pray for members of our community, friends and loved ones
who are ill, especially ....
Show us the path of life.
Lord, hear us, graciously hear us.

We rejoice with all your faithful people, and pray you will make
us to be numbered with your saints in that glory which is
everlasting.
We pray for benefactors, for friends and loved ones departed.
Show us the path of life.
Lord, hear us, graciously hear us.

Keep your eyes fixed on Jesus who is the Way, the Truth and
the Life, that you may walk in the path of peace.
The peace of the Lord be always with you
and also with you.

The Holy Spirit fill your whole being, that you may walk in the
way of love, joy and peace, and glorify the Lord in the beauty of
holiness; and the blessing...

Proper 9

Sunday between 3 and 9 July inclusive

Track 1
2 Kings 5. 1–14
Ps. 30
Galatians 6. [1–6] 7–16
Luke 10. 1–11, 16–20

Track 2
Isaiah 66. 10–14
Ps. 66. 1–9
Galatians 6. [1–6] 7–16
Luke 10. 1–11, 16–20

Almighty God, keep us strong in the faith. Direct us in all our
doings and give us your help, that we may proclaim the glory of
your kingdom, share your peace with those we meet and
continue to rejoice in your saving power; through Jesus Christ
our Lord, who is alive and reigns with you, O Father, and the
Holy Spirit, world without end. **Amen.**

Lord God of all creation, guide us as we strive to serve you,
give us joy in our work and hope for a good outcome.
We pray for all who work as labourers in your harvest:
may they draw others to you rather than themselves;
give them grace to speak out against the wrong and to support
   what is right and good.
Give to all who work in mission and ministry the gift of
   discernment.
Lord of all creation,
let your kingdom come in us.

We give thanks for the wealth and the harvest of the world.
We pray that none may hunger or be deprived,
that the produce and goods of the world may be shared with
   justice.
We remember areas where crops have failed, where people have
   been driven out of their homeland.
Lord of all creation,
let your kingdom come in us.

We give thanks for all that you have given to us;
teach us to be generous and to share with others.
Let us never tire of doing good works.
We pray for our places of work and where we fulfil ourselves.
We remember all who are unemployed and live in poverty.
Lord of all creation,
let your kingdom come in us.

We pray for all who have never been able to work or who have
   lost their employment through illness.
We remember all who suffer from leprosy, all who are
   disfigured, all who are restricted in their movements and
   ability.
We pray especially for any who have suffered from rejection or
   abuse.
We ask your blessing on friends and loved ones who are in
   need.

Lord of all creation,
let your kingdom come in us.

We pray for all who mourn, all who are bereaved, all who are
    grieving.
We remember especially any left on their own and finding it
    hard to cope.
We ask your blessing on our loved ones who are renewed in
    your kingdom.
Lord of all creation,
let your kingdom come in us.

THE PEACE

Rejoice that your names are written in heaven.
Christ has gone to prepare a place for you,
that you may abide with him in his peace.
The peace of the Lord be always with you
and also with you.

THE BLESSING

God fill your hearts with his love,
give you courage to proclaim his kingdom;
and the blessing...

Proper 10

Sunday between 10 and 16 July inclusive

Track 1
Amos 7. 7–17
Ps. 82
Colossians 1. 1–14
Luke 10. 25–37

Track 2
Deuteronomy 30. 9–14
Ps. 25. 1–10
Colossians 1. 1–14
Luke 10. 25–37

Holy and ever-loving God, you bind up our wounds, heal our sickness and restore us to wholeness; make us sensitive to all who are in need or trouble, that we may care for the suffering and be generous in our dealings; through Jesus Christ our Lord, who is alive and reigns with you, O Father, and the Holy Spirit, one God, world without end. **Amen.**

We give you thanks for all who have given us help when we
    were down, for all who have supported us and protected us.
We pray that your church may seek out and recover the fallen,
that we may never avoid our responsibility and pass by on the
    other side.
We pray today for the work of the Salvation Army, for city
    missions and for the work of the Samaritans.
Lord of compassion and love,
deliver us from all evil.

We pray for all who have fallen among thieves,
all who are robbed of their possessions or well-being,
for people robbed of their livelihood or their health.
We remember all who are treated like slave labour,

all who are counted as disposable units.
We pray especially for any who have recently been made
    redundant or homeless.
Lord of compassion and love,
deliver us from all evil.

We give thanks for all who look after our well-being, who
    protect us and seek to supply our needs.
We ask you to bless our homes with your love;
may they be places of gentleness and grace where all are
    accepted and cared for.
We pray for homes where there is violence and cruelty, for
    homes where people live in fear and anxiety.
Lord of compassion and love,
deliver us from all evil.

We give thanks for the work of the emergency services and ask
    your blessing upon the fire service, ambulance workers, the
    police and social workers.
We pray for all carers and especially for doctors and nurses.
We remember all who are down at this time, and all near to
    death, especially if they are lonely and afraid.
We pray for friends who are ill,
    especially ....
Lord of compassion and love,
deliver us from all evil.

We pray that when we are close to death, we know that you
    come to us, O Lord.
We give thanks for all that you have rescued from the valley of
    the shadow of death.
We remember those of our community and our loved ones who
    are in the fullness of eternal life.
Lord of compassion and love,
deliver us from all evil.

He has rescued us from the powers of darkness and brought us into the glory of his kingdom; in him we have redemption and peace.
The peace of the Lord be always with you
and also with you.

THE BLESSING

God give his strength to your weakness.
Christ redeem you from the power of death.
The Holy Spirit refresh and restore you.
And the blessing . . .

Proper 11

Sunday between 17 and 23 July inclusive

———

Track 1	*Track 2*
Amos 8. 1–12	Genesis 18. 1–10a
Ps. 52	Ps. 15
Colossians 1. 15–28	Colossians 1. 15–28
Luke 10. 38–42	Luke 10. 38–42

Lord, among the busyness and bustle of the world,
make us to be still and attentive to your presence;
keep our ears open to your call,
keep our hearts open to your love,
make our minds sensitive to your coming,
that we may ever rejoice that we dwell in you and you are in us;

through Jesus Christ our Lord,
who lives and reigns with you and the Holy Spirit,
one God, now and for ever. **Amen.**

Lord of hosts and hospitality, teach us to be welcoming, open
and friendly.
May your church be attentive to the needs of strangers and
visitors;
may each church be welcoming and friendly and so reflect your
love.
We pray for churches that are struggling because of opposition,
for churches that strive to serve in areas where there is apathy
and animosity.
We remember all who are persecuted for their faith.
God of grace and goodness,
keep us in your peace.

We ask you to bless all who are overworked, stressed and
over-anxious;
we remember especially those who have no time for their homes
or for leisure.
We pray for the work-weary, the exhausted and the worn out.
We remember children who rarely see their parents and who
lack affection.
We pray for all who are restless and cannot enjoy where they
are.
God of grace and goodness,
keep us in your peace.

We give thanks for our homes, for places of peace and quiet, for
places of leisure and recreation.
We pray for all who help us to relax: for musicians, artists,
broadcasters and sportsmen and sportswomen.
We pray for our friends and our loved ones.
God of grace and goodness,
keep us in your peace.

We ask for peace upon all agitated and distressed peoples and
communities.
We remember before you all who feel neglected or ignored, all
lonely and troubled people.
We pray for all who have been misused or abused by others,
all who have suffered from traumatic events, all who have
witnessed horror.
We ask that our friends and loved ones who are ill may know
your love and protection.
God of grace and goodness,
keep us in your peace.

We give thanks for those who are at rest in you, who have
found new peace and new life.
We give thanks for the saints and pray that our loved ones
departed may share with them in that glory which is
everlasting.
God of grace and goodness,
keep us in your peace.

THE PEACE

Be still and accept the peace that God's presence brings:
peace in your hearts,
peace in your minds,
peace in all your dealings.
The peace of the Lord be always with you
and also with you.

THE BLESSING

The peace of God the Father be about you.
The peace of Christ the Son be around you.
The peace of the Holy Spirit be with you.
And the blessing . . .

Proper 12

Sunday between 24 and 30 July inclusive

———

Track 1	*Track 2*
Hosea 1. 2–10	Genesis 18. 20–32
Ps. 85. 1–7 [8–13]	Ps. 138
Colossians 2. 6–15 [16–19]	Colossians 2. 6–15 [16–19]
Luke 11. 1–13	Luke 11. 1–13

Almighty God, our hearts long for you, our spirits yearn for
  you;
we desire to know your presence, we seek your face.
Open our eyes to behold your coming,
cleanse our minds to accept your presence,
touch our hearts to accept your love,
that we may give ourselves in love to you as you give yourself
  to us;
through Jesus Christ our Lord,
who lives and reigns with you and the Holy Spirit,
one God, now and for ever. **Amen.**

Lord, we seek common union with you;
we long to be rooted and grounded in you and your love.
May your whole church show its unity and love in you.
We pray for all who are learning to pray,
all who are being taught to meditate and to contemplate your
  presence.
We pray for religious communities, for spiritual guides and
  counsellors.

Holy God, protect us
and deliver us from all evil.

We pray for all whose lives are absorbed by trivial pursuits,
for all who are possessed by their possessions,
for all who have become addicted, for those caught up in crime.
We remember especially young people who are being led astray.
We pray for all people who have a low esteem of themselves,
    and those who are devalued by others.
Holy God, protect us
and deliver us from all evil.

We give thanks for all who have encouraged us and given us
    confidence,
for all who have helped us to develop our talents and abilities.
We pray for teachers and all who are involved in the
    development of people.
We ask you to bless our homes and our loved ones;
we remember homes where there is neglect and apathy.
Holy God, protect us
and deliver us from all evil.

We ask you to guide and strengthen all who are fearful.
We pray for any who are awaiting a doctor's diagnosis,
all who are awaiting operations or admission to hospital.
We pray for the loved ones of those who are ill and all carers.
We bring before you any we know by name who are
    ill ....
Holy God, protect us
and deliver us from all evil.

Lord, we trust in you and in your power to save.
You are our strength in times of weakness, our hope in times of
    darkness.
We ask you to bless all our loved ones departed and keep them
    in eternal life.

Holy God, protect us
and deliver us from all evil.

THE PEACE

Our God is a very present help in trouble,
he will guide us into the ways of peace.
The peace of the Lord be always with you
and also with you.

THE BLESSING

The almighty God protect you from all evil.
The loving God give you his peace.
The gracious God guide you in your travels.
And the blessing...

Proper 13

Sunday between 31 July and 6 August inclusive

Track 1	*Track 2*
Hosea 11. 1–11	Ecclesiastes 1. 2, 12–14; 2. 18–23
Ps. 107. 1–9 [43]	Ps. 49. 1–9 [10–12]
Colossians 3. 1–11	Colossians 3. 1–11
Luke 12. 13–21	Luke 12. 13–21

O God, from whom all good things come,
give us grace to live to your glory;
give us respect for each other and for all your creation;

fill our lives with a sense of wonder,
and give us wisdom in all our dealings;
through Jesus Christ our Lord,
who is alive and reigns with you and the Holy Spirit,
one God, now and for ever. **Amen.**

All things come from you, O Lord, all goodness and good gifts:
may we see your love and grace in all that is about us;
help us to enjoy the world with the great love that you have for
    the world.
May your church be seen as good stewards of your creation,
using its resources to the benefit of others and to your glory.
We pray for the work of Christian Aid and all relief
    organizations.
Lord of all creation,
keep us in your love.

We pray that we will all remember that life cannot be bought or
    sold.
We remember all who are not paid fairly for their work.
We pray for places of deprivation, the world's poor,
for street children and dwellers in shanty towns,
for nations that are suffering from bankruptcy.
We ask you to bless all who are working for fair trade and
    justice.
Lord of all creation,
keep us in your love.

We give thanks for all that you have given to us;
may we use what we have received for the benefit of others and
    to your glory.
We pray for all who have enriched our lives by their care and
    generosity.
Bless our homes and our loved ones, keep us in your peace.
May the community in which we live be an accepting and
    hospitable community.

Lord of all creation,
keep us in your love.

Lord of all goodness, we remember before you all suffering
    peoples: the war-torn and the weary, the malnourished and
    the starving, all driven out of their homes and off their land
    by the greed of others, all who have been robbed of their
    livelihood or their health.
We pray for friends and loved ones in difficulty at this time,
    remembering all who are ill or unable to cope on their own.
Lord of all creation,
keep us in your love.

We give thanks for all who, though poor in the eyes of the
    world, are precious in your sight.
We pray for all who have departed this life, remembering before
    you especially ....
Lord of all creation,
keep us in your love.

THE PEACE

If you have been raised with Christ, seek the things that are
above.
The peace of the Lord be always with you
and also with you.

THE BLESSING

God, the gracious giver of all good gifts, guide you into the
ways of goodness and generosity; and the blessing...

Proper 14

Sunday between 7 and 13 August inclusive

———

Track 1
Isaiah 1. 1, 10–20
Ps. 50. 1–7 [8, 22–23]
Hebrews 11. 1–3, 8–16
Luke 12. 32–40

Track 2
Genesis 15. 1–6
Ps. 33. 12–21 [22]
Hebrews 11. 1–3, 8–16
Luke 12. 32–40

Holy God, make us aware of your coming to us,
make us sensitive to your presence and alert to your call,
that we may know that we dwell in you and you in us,
and that we may give ourselves to you in love and service;
through Jesus Christ our Lord,
who is alive and reigns with you and the Holy Spirit,
one God, now and for ever. **Amen.**

Lord, we come to you for guidance.
We pray for pilgrims and seekers, all who strive for a better
    world.
We ask your blessing on all who are seeking to extend their
    vision, their sensitivities or their horizon.
We remember all who are seeking to live disciplined lives,
all who are new to the faith, all who are learning of you.
Lord, guide all who in the church are leaders and teachers.
Lord, we put our trust in you.
You are our hope and salvation.

We give thanks for all who have built up our world:
we pray for builders and architects, for city planners and

members of government, for genetic engineers and all
    research workers.
Lord, give us the wisdom to build on firm foundations.
We ask your blessing upon all who live in poverty,
those who live in squalid surroundings,
all who live without much hope or vision.
Lord, we put our trust in you.
You are our hope and salvation.

We give you thanks for all who have extended our vision,
who have increased our capacity to understand and to love.
We pray for all who have shared their vision with us,
for preachers and teachers, for artists and craftspeople,
for our friends and our loved ones.
Lord, we put our trust in you.
You are our hope and salvation.

We pray for all whose vision and abilities are restricted through
    illness or weakness.
We remember all who are losing mobility or agility, all who
    suffer from a stroke or multiple sclerosis, especially those
    who find it hard to communicate, and those who cannot look
    after themselves.
We pray for loved ones who are ill.
Lord, we put our trust in you.
You are our hope and salvation.

You, Lord, will bring us to the Promised Land where sorrow
    and pain are no more, but life and joy are everlasting.
We come to you and seek your blessing upon our loved ones
    who have entered into the fullness of your peace.
Lord, we put our trust in you.
You are our hope and salvation.

The Lord is your hope and your peace.
The Lord is your strength and your salvation.
The peace of the Lord be always with you
and also with you.

THE BLESSING

God the Creator guide you in all that you do.
Christ the Saviour protect you in every journey.
The Spirit of God give you strength for each day.
And the blessing . . .

Proper 15

Sunday between 14 and 20 August inclusive

―――――

Track 1	Track 2
Isaiah 5. 1–7	Jeremiah 23. 23–29
Ps. 80. [1–2] 8–19	Ps. 82
Hebrews 11.29 – 12.2	Hebrews 11.29 – 12.2
Luke 12. 49–56	Luke 12. 49–56

O God, our Father, among the many distractions of the world,
keep our eyes, our minds, our hearts fixed on our Lord Jesus
Christ, the pioneer and perfecter of our faith, that at the last we
may come to the fullness of your eternal kingdom; through the
same Christ our Lord, who lives and reigns with you and the
Holy Spirit, one God, world without end. **Amen.**

We give thanks that we share in the inheritance of your saints.
Grant us and your whole church a spirit of discipline and
    perseverance,
let us not grow slack in well-doing or in our devotion to you.
Lord, make us a holy church, a healing church, a hospitable
    church.
We pray for all who are new to the faith, the newly baptized,
    and the newly confirmed.
We remember any whose faith is wavering or who have lost
    vision.
Holy and Mighty God,
we keep our hope fixed on you.

Lord of righteousness, we pray for fair dealing and justice in
    our world:
we remember before you all involved in commerce and world
    trade.
We pray that the multinational companies may deal with
    integrity, and with respect for all.
We ask that all captives to debt and corruption may find freedom.
Holy and Mighty God,
we keep our hope fixed on you.

We pray for all who work to provide us with our daily needs:
we remember all who work in the service industries, all who
    supply us with food, heat, light and shelter.
We ask your blessing upon our loved ones and friends, upon
    our neighbourhood and our places of work.
Holy and Mighty God,
we keep our hope fixed on you.

God of power, we pray for all exhausted people, and for people
    who live in areas where the land or resources are exhausted.
We remember before you all who are weary and worn, all too
    tired to enjoy life.
We pray for those who are suffering from a breakdown, all who
    cannot cope.

We pray for friends and loved ones who are in trouble or who
   are ill.
Holy and Mighty God,
we keep our hope fixed on you.

Lord, we give thanks that you renew, refresh and restore us;
we pray for all who have passed through the shadow of death
   and entered life and light everlasting.
Holy and Mighty God,
we keep our hope fixed on you.

THE PEACE

Seek for peace, pray for peace,
think of peace, speak of peace,
act in peace, live in peace.
The peace of the Lord be always with you
and also with you.

THE BLESSING

The Almighty God give you strength to run the race that is set
before you, give you power and hope to persevere to the end;
and the blessing . . .

Proper 16

Sunday between 21 and 27 August inclusive

Track 1
Jeremiah 1. 4–10
Ps. 71. 1–6
Hebrews 12. 18–29
Luke 13. 10–17

Track 2
Isaiah 58. 9b-14
Ps. 103. 1–8
Hebrews 12. 18–29
Luke 13. 10–17

Gracious God, open our eyes and extend our vision:
let us see what you would have us do,
what we are capable of and what we can do now.
As you call us and empower us, make us worthy of our calling;
through Jesus Christ our Lord,
who lives and reigns with you and the Holy Spirit,
one God, now and for ever. **Amen.**

Lord, move us, move our wills and direct us by your Spirit.
Help us and your whole church to know when to pull down and
    when to rebuild;
give us discernment and courage to do what you would have
    us do.
We pray for churches and communities caught up in constant
    change,
for those who have become restless and cannot settle at all.
We pray for builders-up of communities and confidence,
for our own pastors and leaders.
Lord, let your light shine upon us
and dispel our darkness.

We pray for all who seek to provide good housing and places of
beauty,
for city planners, architects and builders, for all who maintain
parks and gardens.
We remember all who live in areas of poverty and deprivation,
for all whose lives are in danger through not having clean water
or proper health care.
God bless all who give their lives in the building up of
communities.
Lord, let your light shine upon us
and dispel our darkness.

Lord, teach us to reverence the earth,
to have respect and awe towards each other,
to keep holy days, that we may be aware of you.
We pray for all who have been humiliated and have lost respect
for themselves or others.
We ask you to make our homes places of light and love, of grace
and goodness.
Lord, let your light shine upon us
and dispel our darkness.

We remember all who live in fear through war, oppression or
violence,
all who have suffered from abuse or contempt.
We pray for all who have a poor opinion of themselves.
We ask your blessing on all whose lives are darkened by
crippling illness,
all who are afraid to venture, all who are unable to venture.
We pray for friends and loved ones who are suffering at this
time.
Lord, let your light shine upon us
and dispel our darkness.

We give thanks that you are the God who makes all things new,
you heal and restore your people.

We pray for loved ones who have passed through death and are
   in light and life everlasting.
Lord, let your light shine upon us
and dispel our darkness.

THE PEACE

The Lord forgives all your sin, heals all your infirmities;
he redeems your life from the grave and crowns you with mercy
and loving kindness.
The peace of the Lord be always with you
and also with you.

THE BLESSING

The power of the Almighty Father uphold you.
The presence of Christ the Redeemer restore you.
The peace of the Holy Spirit be about you.
And the blessing . . .

Proper 17

Sunday between 28 August and 3 September inclusive

―――――

Track 1
Jeremiah 2. 4–13
Ps. 81. 1, 10–16 (*or* 1–11)
Hebrews 13. 1–8, 15–16
Luke 14. 1, 7–14

Track 2
Ecclesiasticus 10. 12–18
or Proverbs 25. 6–7
Ps. 112
Hebrews 13. 1–8, 15–16
Luke 14. 1, 7–14

Gracious God, you are always more ready to hear us than we are to pray, and you give us more than we either desire or deserve. May we remember that all our gifts, abilities and life come from you, and grant that we may use them to your glory and to the benefit of others; through Jesus Christ our Lord, who is alive and reigns with you and the Holy Spirit, one God, now and for ever. **Amen.**

Lord, it is you and your call that gives us dignity or position; without you we would be nothing, we would not even exist. Forgive us false pride and those times we seek to be
protectionist, when we jockey for position or belittle others.
Give your church true humility and a sense of hospitality to all.
We pray for those who preach and evangelize in areas of
poverty, apathy or animosity, for all who face humiliation for their faith.
We remember all who have lost their way and are no longer fulfilling their vocation.
Lord, as you call us,
make us worthy of our calling.

116

We give thanks for all who care for the homeless and the
    destitute:
we pray for social workers and all who seek to help others in
    their needs.
We remember the relief agencies and the World Health
    Organization,
the work of the Red Cross, and all who care for refugees.
Lord, as you call us,
make us worthy of our calling.

We give thanks for all who have welcomed us into their homes,
all who have been hospitable, all who have shown us love.
We pray for family life and the sanctity of marriage.
We remember all who are suffering from a breakdown in their
    relationships.
We ask that we may learn contentment and avoid greed.
Lord, as you call us,
make us worthy of our calling.

We remember all who have been belittled by others,
all who have no confidence in themselves, the timid and
    nervous.
We ask your blessing upon all who live in hostile areas, in
    places of war, oppression, or abuse.
We remember all who are ill, especially ....
Lord, as you call us,
make us worthy of our calling.

We give thanks that you invite us and accept us into your
    kingdom,
that you have triumphed over death and offer us life eternal.
We pray for loved ones and friends in
    eternity ....
Lord, as you call us,
make us worthy of our calling.

Let mutual love continue and do not forget to show hospitality.
The peace of the Lord be always with you
and also with you.

Do not neglect to do good and share what you have, for such
sacrifices are pleasing to God; and the blessing . . .

Proper 18

Sunday between 4 and 10 September inclusive

———

Track 1
Jeremiah 18. 1–11
Ps. 139. 1–6, 13–18 (*or* 1–8)
Philemon 1–21
Luke 14. 25–33

Track 2
Deuteronomy 30. 15–20
Ps. 1
Philemon 1–21
Luke 14. 25–33

God of time and space,
you call us to discern your presence in the world:
grant us wisdom to perceive you,
grant us courage to work with you,
grant us power to proclaim you,
above all grant us a heart to love you;
through Jesus Christ our Lord,
who is alive and reigns with you and the Holy Spirit,
one God, now and for ever. **Amen.**

Lord God, in our freedom guide us,
that we may choose love and not hatred,
that we may choose light rather than darkness,
that we may choose life and not death,
that we may turn freely to you, and so abide for ever.
Grant your church courage to proclaim the gospel and to reveal
    your glory in the way we live.
Loving God, guide us
and grant us a glimpse of your glory.

We pray for all people who are confused in a world of
    multi-choice,
for all who lack clear direction, and all who are led astray.
We pray that the leaders in our world and in the media may set
    good examples.
We remember especially those who teach the young and
    influence them.
We pray for youth leaders and all who deal with growing people.
Loving God, guide us
and grant us a glimpse of your glory.

We give thanks for our own homes and loved ones, and ask you
    to bless them with your love and peace.
We pray for the newly married, and for those looking after
    children;
we ask your blessing on nursery classes and all child-minders.
Loving God, guide us
and grant us a glimpse of your glory.

We pray for people whose lives are insecure,
all whose relationships, homes or work are at risk;
we pray for all who have become captive to vice and drugs.
We ask your blessing on all whose health is failing,
on those whose powers are waning and are becoming
    dependent on others.
Lord, give strength and courage to loved ones who are ill,
    especially ....

Loving God, guide us
and grant us a glimpse of your glory.

We give thanks for the promise of eternal life and the hope of
   glory,
for the saints who are in your kingdom.
We pray for loved ones and friends who are departed from us.
Loving God, guide us
and grant us a glimpse of your glory.

THE PEACE

Grace to you and peace from God the Creator.
Goodness to you and peace from Christ the Redeemer.
Guidance to you and peace from the Holy Spirit of God.
The peace of the Lord be always with you
and also with you.

THE BLESSING

God give you grace and guide you, that you may work with
Christ, and so do the will and the wonderful works of God; and
the blessing . . .

Proper 19

Sunday between 11 and 17 September inclusive

Track 1
Jeremiah 4. 11–12, 22–28
Ps. 14
1 Timothy 1. 12–17
Luke 15. 1–10

Track 2
Exodus 32. 7–14
Ps. 51. 1–10
1 Timothy 1. 12–17
Luke 15. 1–10

Good and gracious Shepherd,
we rejoice in your protection and care,
we know you will seek us out and save us:
guide us, O Lord, and keep us in the ways that lead to peace;
through Jesus Christ our Lord,
who is alive and reigns with you and the Holy Spirit,
one God, now and for ever. **Amen.**

Lord God, you come and seek us out,
you call us and empower us to live to your glory,
you are our Shepherd and guide, you are our God.
We pray for all who have strayed from the faith, all who have
    got lost in various ways, especially any whose lives are in
    danger.
We pray for shepherds of your flock, for all ministers, pastors,
    bishops, priests and deacons.
Good and faithful Shepherd,
guide us into the ways of life and peace.

God our protector, we remember before you all who work or
    live in dangerous places or a hostile environment, all who are

suffering at this time from storms and disasters, all who are caught up in strife and warfare.
We pray for all who are seeking peace and well-being for the world:
we remember the United Nations and peace-keeping forces.
Good and faithful Shepherd,
guide us into the ways of life and peace.

Lord, we give thanks for all who have sought us out in times of troubles, who have been a strength and a joy to us.
We pray that you will guide all who teach and influence others.
Let us know your presence in our homes and with our loved ones.
Guide us in our choices and in our friendships.
Good and faithful Shepherd,
guide us into the ways of life and peace.

We ask you to be with all who walk in darkness:
may your love and light protect the depressed and despairing;
may your strength and hope be known to the discouraged.
We ask your blessing upon all who are ill at home or in hospital;
we remember especially ....
Good and faithful Shepherd,
guide us into the ways of life and peace.

We pray for all who are entering the shadow of death and for their loved ones in their time of anxiety.
Bless all who are in a hospice and all who have the care of the terminally ill.
We pray for all who have passed through death and entered life eternal.
Good and faithful Shepherd,
guide us into the ways of life and peace.

Christ, the Good Shepherd, seeks out those who are lost until he
    finds them and brings them home and to peace.
The peace of the Lord be always with you
and also with you.

THE BLESSING

God, who cares for you as a shepherd cares for his sheep,
protect you.
Christ, the Good Shepherd, who seeks out and saves the lost, be
with you.
The Holy Spirit of God, who is your Guide, lead you into the
ways of peace.
And the blessing . . .

Proper 20

Sunday between 18 and 24 September inclusive

Track 1	Track 2
Jeremiah 8.18 – 9.1	Amos 8. 4–7
Ps. 79. 1–9	Ps. 113
1 Timothy 2. 1–7	1 Timothy 2. 1–7
Luke 16. 1–13	Luke 16. 1–13

Holy God, as you have called us to serve you, guide us and
make us worthy of our calling. Give us wisdom to use our
talents and resources to your glory and the benefit of all who
are in need; through Jesus Christ our Lord, who is alive and

reigns with you and the Holy Spirit, one God, now and for ever.
Amen.

Father, we give you thanks for your love and forgiveness.
Teach us to forgive as you have forgiven us,
to be merciful and yet to maintain justice.
We pray for all penitents, all who seek forgiveness.
Lord, guide all who are spiritual counsellors and confessors.
We pray for all who lead retreats and who look after conference
  centres.
Help us, O Lord our God.
Save us for the glory of your Name.

We ask you to strengthen and guide all who are in positions of
  trust, all in places of authority, all who make decisions
  concerning our future.
We pray for integrity and fair dealing in world trade, that no
  one is counted as cheap labour or as of little importance.
We remember all who are impoverished, all who cry for justice,
  all who work for freedom and dignity.
Help us, O Lord our God.
Save us for the glory of your Name.

We give thanks for all you have given to us.
We ask you to bless our homes and families with your presence,
  love and peace.
We pray for homes where there is unrest, fearfulness and
  violence, for all who have suffered abuse or neglect, for
  children taken into care and for those who are left at risk.
Help us, O Lord our God.
Save us for the glory of your Name.

We remember before you all whose wounds find no cure.
We pray for the chronically ill, the pathologically disturbed, for
  all who suffer from schizophrenia, all who are deeply
  distressed, any who are troubled in body, mind or spirit.
We remember loved ones who are ill at this time.

Help us, O Lord our God.
Save us for the glory of your Name.

We give thanks for all who have triumphed over the troubles of
    this world and are now at rest and at peace in your kingdom.
We pray for friends and loved ones departed from us.
Help us, O Lord our God.
Save us for the glory of your Name.

THE PEACE

Christ Jesus, himself human, gave his life as ransom for all, that
in him we may find newness of life, forgiveness and peace.
The peace of the Lord be always with you
and also with you.

THE BLESSING

May your life be filled with dignity and peace,
your heart with the joy and love of the Lord;
and the blessing . . .

Proper 21

Sunday between 25 September and 1 October inclusive

Track 1
Jeremiah 32. 1–3a, 6–15
Ps. 91. 1–6, 14–16 (*or* 11–16)
1 Timothy 6. 6–19
Luke 16. 19–31

Track 2
Amos 6. 1a, 4–7
Ps. 146
1 Timothy 6. 6–19
Luke 16. 19–31

Good and gracious God, all that we have comes from you;
make us sensitive in all our dealings with each other and with
   your whole creation.
Grant that we may reflect your generosity in our lives and do
   your will here on earth,
that we may come to rejoice in your heavenly kingdom;
through Jesus Christ our Lord,
who is alive and reigns with you and the Holy Spirit,
one God, world without end. **Amen.**

Lord, the Creator of all, give us a sense of respect for all people:
let your church work for the good of all and the uplifting of
   those who are down.
We pray for all relief organizations, for those working among
   the world's poor.
We remember the church in its work in shanty towns and
   among street children.
Lord, guide us that we may be good stewards of what you have
   given to us.
Lord, make us loving people
and a caring people.

We pray for all who work for little wages and live in poverty:
all who are misused and cheated in the world of trade.
We pray for countries in deep debt, for places of famine and
  hunger.
We remember all whose homes and land have been spoiled by
  war, by a lack of respect for the earth, by the greed of
  multinationals;
for all who are losing their heritage through the power of
  others.
Lord, make us loving people
and a caring people.

We give thanks for all who taught us love by loving us,
for those who gave us respect for ourselves and confidence.
Lord, teach us to be open to the needs of others in our homes
  and in our communities:
let us not become hardened or neglectful.
We pray for homes where there is no respect for each other,
where there is neglect and apathy, where there is abuse and
  animosity.
Lord, make us loving people
and a caring people.

We pray for all who lack well-being, the ill at home or in
  hospital.
We remember those who have no home or security, who have
  no one to care for them.
We pray for all who suffer through feeling unwanted or rejected,
all who have been betrayed in love, all who have been deserted.
We pray for friends and loved ones in their needs,
for all ill and suffering people, especially ....
Lord, make us loving people
and a caring people.

We give thanks for all who have entered the fullness of joy and
  peace in your kingdom,
for all who are refreshed and restored in your kingdom.

We ask you to bless friends and loved ones departed,
especially ....
Lord, make us loving people
and a caring people.

THE PEACE

Do good, be rich in good works, generous and ready to share,
live in peace with all.
The peace of the Lord be always with you
and also with you.

THE BLESSING

Grace, mercy and peace be yours, from God who abounds in
love for you and all people; and the blessing...

Proper 22

Sunday between 2 and 8 October inclusive

———

Track 1
Lamentations 1. 1–6
Canticle: Lamentations 3. 19–26
or Ps. 137. 1–6 [7–9]
2 Timothy 1. 1–14
Luke 17. 5–10

Track 2
Habakkuk 1. 1–4; 2. 1–4
Ps. 37. 1–9
2 Timothy 1. 1–14
Luke 17. 5–10

O merciful God, by your grace you have called us,
not as we deserve but in your goodness and generosity;
guard and protect us in our calling,

that we may be strong in the faith and serve you in joy and love;
through Jesus Christ our Lord,
who is alive and reigns with you and the Holy Spirit,
one God, now and for ever. **Amen.**

Lord, we rejoice in your love and care, you accept us and
    restore us.
We pray for the healing ministry of the church,
for faith healers and for groups that meet to pray for healing,
for all who bless others through the laying on of hands.
We pray for the work of the church with the healing
    professions:
we remember hospital chaplains and those who visit the infirm.
We pray for the Guild of Health and the Guild of St Raphael.
Lord, we come to you.
You alone can make us whole.

We pray for the healing of the nations,
for the cure of past hurts, for forgiveness of past sins,
that all may take the opportunity of a new start,
that animosity may be exchanged for trust and love.
We remember communities broken by war, hatred and
    suspicion;
we pray for those driven out of their land and homes by
    violence.
Lord, we come to you.
You alone can make us whole.

We give thanks for our lives and all we can do.
We pray for our homes and the communities to which we
    belong.
We pray for families who are suffering from a breakdown in
    their relationships, for children who suffer and for those
    taken into care.
We pray for the broken-hearted and the lonely.
Lord, we come to you.
You alone can make us whole.

We ask you to bless all who are disorientated, or distressed,
all who are suffering from a breakdown of their well-being.
We bring before you all who will go into hospital or care today,
all who suffer from strokes, heart attacks or sudden illness;
we remember those who are chronically ill.
We pray for friends and loved ones in their needs.
Lord, we come to you.
You alone can make us whole.

We give thanks for all who have passed through brokenness to
    new life in glory, where sorrow and pain are no more.
We pray for loved ones who have entered into eternal life.
Lord, we come to you.
You alone can make us whole.

THE PEACE

The deep love of God never ceases.
The Prince of Peace offers you his peace.
The Spirit of the Lord restores and refreshes you.
The peace of the Lord be always with you
and also with you.

THE BLESSING

The love of God be your strength.
The power of the Saviour be your hope.
The grace of the Spirit be your peace.
And the blessing . . .

Proper 23

Sunday between 9 and 15 October inclusive

———

Track 1
Jeremiah 29. 1, 4–7
Ps. 66. 1–12
2 Timothy 2. 8–15
Luke 17. 11–19

Track 2
2 Kings 5. 1–3, 7–15c
Ps. 111
2 Timothy 2. 8–15
Luke 17. 11–19

Almighty God, whose power is revealed in our weakness, and whose grace meets our every need; we give you thanks for your healing and your love and pray you will guide us always to keep our hope and our trust in you; through Jesus Christ our Lord, who is alive and reigns with you and the Holy Spirit, one God, now and for ever. **Amen.**

Holy and Mighty God, how wonderful is all your creation;
we give you thanks and praise for all you have given to us.
We pray for the work of the church among the scorned and
    rejected, among those who are not easily socially acceptable.
We pray for the church's work among those suffering with
    leprosy, among those with AIDS, among all of whom society
    is afraid or scornful.
We pray for Christians who work in dangerous or lonely places;
we remember those who suffer persecution for their faith.
Lord, you are our hope.
We put our trust in you.

We pray for down-town areas of cities, for areas of deprivation
    and places looked on as ghettos.

We pray for all who are not allowed a fair chance in life because of where they come from or because of their looks.

We remember all areas where there is prejudice and hostility, all places of ethnic fear and animosity.

Lord, you are our hope.

We put our trust in you.

We give thanks for those who have accepted us as we are, and we pray for our friends and our loved ones,

that our communities may be places of peace and mutual love, that we may learn respect for all peoples.

We remember all those who feel rejected and unloved.

Lord, you are our hope.

We put our trust in you.

We pray for all who have been disfigured through accident or illness.

We remember those who suffer through the cruelty and thoughtlessness of others.

We pray for all who are working with people with contagious diseases.

We remember friends and loved ones who are ill at this time.

We pray especially for ....

Lord, you are our hope.

We put our trust in you.

We give thanks that you heal and renew your people.

We pray for loved ones who have been changed into glory,

remembering especially today ....

Lord, you are our hope.

We put our trust in you.

THE PEACE

The Lord is your strength and your salvation, in him alone is wholeness and peace.

The peace of the Lord be always with you
and also with you.

THE BLESSING

The goodness of God the Father go with you.
The grace of our Lord Jesus Christ protect you.
The guidance of the Holy Spirit of God ever lead you.
And the blessing . . .

Proper 24

Sunday between 16 and 22 October inclusive

―――――

Track 1	*Track 2*
Jeremiah 31. 27–34	Genesis 32. 22–31
Ps. 119. 97–104	Ps. 121
2 Timothy 3.14 – 4.5	2 Timothy 3.14 – 4.5
Luke 18. 1–8	Luke 18. 1–8

Loving God, you are always ready to love us and accept us, always more ready to hear than we to pray; teach us to abide in you and know you abide in us, to place ourselves in your presence and your peace and to live and work to your glory; through Jesus Christ our Lord, who is alive and reigns with you and the Holy Spirit, one God, now and for ever. **Amen.**

We give you thanks for all who proclaim your power, peace and presence.
We pray for preachers of the word and ministers of the sacrament, for those who are priests and pastors in our community.

We remember all who are teaching the faith and for those
  seeking to learn more;
we ask you to guide our teachers and to bless us in our learning.
We pray for all being prepared for baptism, for parents and
  Godparents, for those being prepared for confirmation or
  ordination.
Lord, show us your way.
Teach us your path.

We ask your blessing on the judicial system,
we pray for law courts, barristers, lawyers, juries.
We remember all who seek to keep law and order,
we pray for the police and the probation service.
We pray for areas where there is injustice and a lack of freedom,
for all who suffer wrongfully and all who are oppressed.
Lord, show us your way.
Teach us your path.

We give thanks for all who have shared their wisdom and
  learning with us.
We pray for teachers and tutors, for Sunday schools and day
  schools.
We pray that we may learn to listen, be sensitive and open to
  others.
We remember all who are deprived of education, all who are
  indoctrinated, all who have learning difficulties.
We ask you to guide us and our loved ones at all times.
Lord, show us your way.
Teach us your path.

We remember before you all who have lost their way, all who
  have lost their grip on reality, all who are deluding
  themselves or others.
We pray for the confused, the harassed, the dejected, especially
  for any whose minds refuse to cope and those suffering from
  memory loss or Alzheimer's disease.
We remember loved ones who are ill ....

Lord, show us your way.
Teach us your path.

We give thanks that you seek us out and lead us to you and
eternal life.
We remember before you friends and loved ones in your
kingdom.
Lord, show us your way.
Teach us your path.

THE PEACE

The Lord guide you into paths of peace, keep you in the way of
holiness, and strengthen you in his service.
The peace of the Lord be always with you
and also with you.

THE BLESSING

Our help comes from the Lord, the Maker of heaven and earth.
Our hope is in Christ our Saviour and Redeemer.
Our direction comes from the Holy Spirit our Sanctifier and
Guide.
And the blessing . . .

Proper 25

Sunday between 23 and 29 October inclusive

Track 1
Joel 2. 23–32
Ps. 65. 1–8 [9–13]
2 Timothy 4. 6–8, 16–18
Luke 18. 9–14

Track 2
Ecclesiasticus 35. 12–17
or Jeremiah 14. 7–10, 19–22
Ps. 84. 1–7
2 Timothy 4. 6–8, 16–18
Luke 18. 9–14

Holy Father, you hear the prayers of the lowly, and forgive the
  sins of the penitent:
grant us a glimpse of your glory,
a humility in our approach to you,
and a deep awareness of your presence and love;
through Jesus Christ our Lord,
who is alive and reigns with you and the Holy Spirit,
one God, now and for ever. **Amen.**

We give you thanks for the beauty, mystery and wonder of
  creation;
teach us to love the world with the great love that you have for
  the world.
We pray that all within the church may show respect for the
  earth,
that Christians will be deeply involved in conservation and
  caring for the planet.
At the same time, may we know that we are strangers and
  pilgrims on the earth.

We pray for all who are seekers, all who look for purpose and
    meaning, all who teach and guide others in the way.
Lord, restore your people.
Guide us into the ways of peace.

We remember any who have become lost in their journey
    through life, all who are slaves to drugs or caught up in
    crime.
We pray for leaders of nations and peoples, for a right use of
    the wealth and the resources of the earth.
We remember all who are suffering from floods or famine, for
    all where the land is exhausted and crops are failing.
Lord, restore your people.
Guide us into the ways of peace.

We give thanks for our loved ones and all who have cared
    for us.
We pray for all who have taught us to value our lives and each
    other.
We pray for all who have lost vision or hope and have little
    support.
We pray for our families and friends and those among whom
    we work.
Lord, restore your people.
Guide us into the ways of peace.

God of all power, we ask you to support all who are down:
we pray for the exhausted, the weary and the worn, those who
    have run out of energy and all who can no longer cope on
    their own.
We ask your blessing on all who are suffering from depression.
We pray for friends and loved ones who are
    ill . . . .
Lord, restore your people.
Guide us into the ways of peace.

We think of all those who have run the race, finished the course
and kept the faith:
we give thanks for your saints and all holy men and women.
Lord, bless all our loved ones who are departed from us and
keep them in life eternal.
Lord, restore your people.
Guide us into the ways of peace.

THE PEACE

The Lord, the Mighty One, stand by you and give you strength.
The Prince of Peace travel with you and give you peace.
The Spirit of God restore and refresh you.
The peace of the Lord be always with you
and also with you.

THE BLESSING

God the Father enfold you in his love.
Christ the Son deliver you from all evil.
The Holy Spirit inspire and lead you always.
And the blessing . . .

Bible Sunday

Isaiah 45. 22–25 : Ps. 119. 129–136 : Romans 15. 1–6 : Luke 4. 16–24

God of the living word,
open our ears to your message,
open our eyes to see your wonders,

open our hearts to experience your love,
open our minds to your wisdom,
that we may hear and receive your word and obey your holy
    will;
through Jesus Christ the Word made flesh,
who lives and reigns with you and the Holy Spirit,
one God, now and for ever. **Amen.**

We give thanks for the holy Scriptures, for your word revealed
    to us.
We pray that we may study your holy word diligently, and ask
    your blessing on all Bible study groups and their leaders.
We pray for preachers of the word, theologians and Bible
    translators, for all organizations that seek to provide people
    with the Scriptures.
We remember before you all who are growing in the faith, for
    those in confirmation classes and preparation for baptism
    classes.
Lord of the Scriptures,
we put our trust in you.

We pray for all who work to bring in your kingdom, all who
    seek release for captives, to bring sight to the blind, to bind
    up the broken-hearted and to restore the fallen.
We ask your blessing on relief agencies and care workers, for
    the work of the Red Cross and the United Nations.
Lord of the Scriptures,
we put our trust in you.

We give thanks for all who share their wisdom and the
    Scriptures with us.
We pray for friends and loved ones who have lost faith,
for any who have become hard and cynical,
for all who fail to see glimpses of glory, or hear your call.
We pray for our quiet witness to those among whom we live.
Lord of the Scriptures,
we put our trust in you.

We ask your blessing on all who seek to serve you under
  difficulties,
all who are persecuted for their faith, those who are mocked
  and ridiculed, all whose lives are in danger.
We remember all ill and suffering peoples, all those who do not
  know or love you.
We pray for friends and loved ones in their troubles or illness.
Lord of the Scriptures,
we put our trust in you.

We give thanks for all who have heard and obeyed your word,
all who have kept faith and witnessed to your saving power.
We pray for loved ones departed from our midst.
Lord of the Scriptures,
we put our trust in you.

THE PEACE

Let the word of the Lord be a light to your path, peace in your
life, and hope for your journey.
The peace of the Lord be always with you
and also with you.

THE BLESSING

God who created all things by his word, direct you.
Jesus the Word made flesh, dwell among you.
The Holy Spirit of God inspire you to obey his word.
And the blessing . . .

Dedication Festival

The First Sunday in October or Last Sunday after Trinity

———

1 Chronicles 29. 6–19 : Ps. 122 : Ephesians 2. 19–22 : John 2. 13–22

Eternal God, we give you thanks for this church:
here we come to affirm your presence and declare your love;
here we come for healing and renewal;
here we adore you and dedicate ourselves to you.
May all who come here know this is a holy place,
a presence-filled place and that you give yourself to them;
through Jesus Christ our Lord,
who is alive and reigns with you and the Holy Spirit,
one God, now and for ever. **Amen.**

Ever-present and loving God,
we give you thanks for all who have gone before us,
those who built up this church and community,
all who dedicated themselves to you in this holy place.
We pray for all who have been baptized and confirmed here,
all who have been married and found support from here,
all who have been buried from here, and all who have found
    new hope.
We give thanks for all who have ministered in this church,
all who have shared in its mission and outreach, and in its
    maintenance.
We pray for our present minister/priest and the staff and
    workers of this church.

Lord, you have called your people.
Make us worthy of our calling.

We pray for the relationship between our church and the wider
  community,
that we may serve where we are able, that we may relieve
  poverty and suffering.
We pray for Christians involved in government, in politics, in
  all matters that influence our lives.
May we help to keep society caring and sensitive.
Lord, you have called your people.
Make us worthy of our calling.

We give thanks for those who taught us the faith.
We pray for the teachers of this church, its Bible classes,
  confirmation classes, Sunday school, and all who are
  prepared for marriage and baptism.
We pray for house visitors and those who care for the
  housebound and infirm.
Lord, bless our congregation, our homes, our friends and our
  loved ones.
Lord, you have called your people.
Make us worthy of our calling.

We remember all who cannot come to church because of illness
  or circumstance;
we pray for all who share in a house communion, or a house
  group.
We pray for all who are lonely and unvisited.
We ask you to bless and support all who are in weakness or
  distress;
we remember friends and loved ones who are ill,
  especially ....
Lord, you have called your people.
Make us worthy of our calling.

We give thanks for all who once worshipped here and are at one
    with the saints in glory,
all who have found faith here and are now in the fullness of
    your kingdom.
We pray for loved ones departed from us ....
Lord, you have called your people.
Make us worthy of our calling.

THE PEACE

Live in faith and in fellowship with each other:
know God's peace and share God's peace.
The peace of the Lord be always with you
and also with you.

THE BLESSING

God who called you to love him,
make you worthy of your calling;
guide, strengthen and protect you,
and grant you a glimpse of his glory;
and the blessing ...

All Saints' Day

Sunday between 30 October and 5 November or, if this is not kept as All Saints' Sunday, on 1 November itself

———

Daniel 7. 1–3, 15–18 : Ps. 149 : Ephesians 1. 11–23 : Luke 6. 20–31

Holy God, you call us to be holy; we give you thanks and praise for the sanctity of the saints, the virtue of virgins, the perception of the prophets, and the witness of martyrs. May we be inspired by them and live and work to your praise and glory; through Jesus Christ our Lord, who is alive and reigns with you and the Holy Spirit, one God, now and for ever. **Amen.**

We give thanks for all who through faith have built up your
    church, for those who quietly served you and the community;
we remember especially any who have inspired us.
May we become the people you have called us to be, a chosen
    people, a holy people.
May we each fulfil our vocation and use our gifts to your glory
    and the relief of those in need.
Lord, make us to be numbered with your saints
in that glory which is everlasting.

Bless, O Lord, all peace-makers: guide the work of the United
    Nations and all those who are striving for peace and freedom.
We pray for all who seek to promote justice, integrity and right
    dealings, for all who work for fair trade, and all relief
    organizations.
Lord, make us to be numbered with your saints
in that glory which is everlasting.

We give you thanks for all who have inspired us,
who have enriched our lives by their goodness and faith.
We pray for all who are seeking to live a godly and saintly life.
We ask your blessing upon our community, our homes and
loved ones;
we remember before you all who are lonely and fearful.
Lord, make us to be numbered with your saints
in that glory which is everlasting.

We pray for all who watch and wait for your coming,
for the weary and the worn, the hungry and the rejected,
all who long for justice and freedom, all who weep because of
injustice.
We pray for all who suffer for their faith: the scorned and the
persecuted, the mocked and the ignored.
We pray for friends and loved ones who are suffering, that they
may be strong in their faith.
Lord, make us to be numbered with your saints
in that glory which is everlasting.

We give thanks for all who have triumphed in your Name,
all who have been undefeated and undiminished and now share
in the communion of saints in your kingdom.
Lord, make us to be numbered with your saints
in that glory which is everlasting.

THE PEACE

God, who has called you to his presence and his peace, make
you to be numbered with his saints.
The peace of the Lord be always with you
and also with you.

THE BLESSING

God grant you a glimpse of his glory.
Christ lead you to the kingdom of God.
The Holy Spirit sanctify you and fill you with wisdom.
And the blessing . . .

Sundays Before Advent

The Fourth Sunday Before Advent

Sunday between 30 October and 5 November inclusive. For use if the Feast of All Saints was celebrated on 1 November and alternative propers are needed.

———

Isaiah 1. 10–18 : Ps. 32. 1–7 : 2 Thessalonians 1. 1–12 : Luke 19. 1–10

Lord, open our eyes to your glory, that we may know your presence and power, and in knowing you, we may love and serve you and live in righteousness and peace; through Jesus Christ our Lord, who is alive and reigns with you and the Holy Spirit, one God, now and for ever. **Amen.**

Lord, we give thanks that you sought us out and brought us to yourself.
We pray for all who are newcomers to the faith: the newly converted, the baptized, the confirmed;
for all who are seekers and exploring the meaning of life.
Lord, may the church help to show that you seek for and welcome all;
may your church be an accepting church, a hospitable church.
We ask that you will guide us in our stewardship,
that we may use our gifts to the benefit of others and to your glory.

Lord, you seek and save that which is lost.
Have mercy on us and hear our prayer.

We ask your blessing upon all who work in commerce, upon
financiers and bankers, upon tax-collectors and accountants.
We pray for individuals and countries that are deeply in debt,
for the world's poor and for all who have suffered because of
the greed, corruption and deceitfulness of others.
We pray for the liberation of all who are impoverished.
Lord, you seek and save that which is lost.
Have mercy on us and hear our prayer.

We give thanks for generous people, welcoming people, for
those who have enriched our lives by their grace and
goodness.
We pray for our own families and loved ones, for the area in
which we live and the places where we work.
Lord, you seek and save that which is lost.
Have mercy on us and hear our prayer.

We pray for all who have been belittled by others,
all who have been squeezed out of their community,
all who are despised or rejected, all who have to do unpopular
work.
We remember all who are feeling hurt, all who are despairing or
desolate,
all who feel lost and have nowhere or nobody to turn to.
We pray for friends and loved ones suffering at this time.
Lord, you seek and save that which is lost.
Have mercy on us and hear our prayer.

We rejoice that you welcome us into your presence and your
kingdom.
We give thanks for the forgiveness of sins and opportunity to
amend our lives.
We ask your blessing upon all whom you have welcomed in
love and into life eternal, especially ....

147

Lord, you seek and save that which is lost.
Have mercy on us and hear our prayer.

THE PEACE

The grace and goodness of God be given to you;
the power and peace of the presence be all about you.
The peace of the Lord be always with you
and also with you.

THE BLESSING

God give you grace to behold his glory,
to enter into his love,
to be guided by his wisdom;
and the blessing . . .

The Third Sunday Before Advent

Sunday between 6 and 12 November inclusive

———

Job 19. 23–27a : Ps. 17. 1–8 [9] : 2 Thessalonians 2. 1–5, 13–17 : Luke 20. 27–38

Eternal God, you give us love, you give us life, you give us
    yourself;
help us to give our love, our lives, ourselves to you,
that we may dwell in you and you in us;
through Jesus Christ our Lord,

who is alive and reigns with you and the Holy Spirit,
one God, now and for ever. **Amen.**

Holy God, guide your church as it is set among many dangers,
keep it in the ways of truth and peace;
may it stand for justice and righteousness.
We pray for Christians who are being persecuted,
for those edged out of their communities, and those who are
　　imprisoned for their faith.
May we and the church to which we belong be faithful to you
　　and ready to serve those who are in need.
Lord, keep us under your protection.
Deliver us from all that is evil.

We pray for all whose lives are at risk: the men and women of
　　the armed forces keeping peace, the police, the men and
　　women of the fire service, all who attend accidents and
　　disasters, paramedics and doctors.
We ask your blessing on all travellers and all who are in danger
　　at this time.
Lord, keep us under your protection.
Deliver us from all that is evil.

We give thanks for the security of our homes.
Protect all who have lost their homes through debt or disaster.
Guide all who are having difficulties in their relationships, all
　　whose márriages or families are breaking down.
We pray for all who seek to give their lives in love and service.
Lord, keep us under your protection.
Deliver us from all that is evil.

We remember before you all who are finding life a problem,
all who are disillusioned, discouraged or despairing,
all who are without vision or hope.
Bless all involved in accidents or who are taken ill today;
we remember the chronically ill and the dying.
We pray for loved ones in their need.

Lord, keep us under your protection.
Deliver us from all that is evil.

We give thanks that you bear us up and do not suffer us to face
destruction; you offer us life which is eternal.
We pray for loved ones departed, for all who have left sorrow
and pain for life and love eternal.
Lord, keep us under your protection.
Deliver us from all that is evil.

THE PEACE

God give you strength for every good work,
give courage to your hearts and peace to your minds.
The peace of the Lord be always with you
and also with you.

THE BLESSING

The Lord keep you as the apple of his eye,
hide you under the protection of his wings.
God's love enfold you,
God's grace go with you,
God's power protect you;
and the blessing . . .

The Second Sunday Before Advent

Sunday between 13 and 19 November inclusive

—————

Malachi 4. 1–2a : Ps. 98 : 2 Thessalonians 3. 6–13 : Luke 21. 5–19

Lord God Almighty,
we look for you, we long for you,
we watch for you, we wait for you.
Give us wisdom to know you and courage to serve you,
whom to serve is perfect freedom;
through Jesus Christ our Lord,
who is alive and reigns with you and the Holy Spirit,
one God, now and for ever. **Amen.**

Lord, we ask you to give strength to all who are weary;
strengthen our faith in times of trouble,
when there are wars and rumours of wars,
when there is famine and earthquake.
May we continue to put our trust in you
and to work for the coming of your kingdom.
We pray for areas where churches are destroyed, vandalized or
    robbed, where priests and pastors are at risk.
The Lord is our strength.
He alone is our salvation.

Lord, guide all who deal with world crises,
protect the peace-keepers and maintainers of the law;
let all who work for justice and freedom know your care.

Give wisdom to the work of the United Nations, the World
Health Organization, and the Save the Children Fund.
The Lord is our strength.
He alone is our salvation.

We pray for homes where it is hard to be a Christian, where
there is enmity and strife and violence, for homes where there
is neglect and abuse.
We give thanks for all agencies and people that support families
in their needs.
We pray for our own homes and loved ones.
The Lord is our strength.
He alone is our salvation.

We pray for all who are victims of war, earthquake, floods,
famine, poverty, injustice and tyranny; for the homeless and
the unemployed.
We remember all who have lost vision and hope.
We pray for all who are ill at home or in hospital,
especially . . . .
The Lord is our strength.
He alone is our salvation.

We give thanks for the coming of your kingdom:
love will triumph over hatred, war will be no more.
We pray for all who have entered into the fullness of your glory
and for all our loved ones departed.
The Lord is our strength.
He alone is our salvation.

THE PEACE

The Lord keep you from all evil, deliver you from all troubles,
and guide you into the ways of peace.
The peace of the Lord be always with you
and also with you.

The glory of God the Father be about you and within you.
The love of Christ our Lord sustain you and fill you.
The power of the Holy Spirit inspire you and guide you.
And the blessing . . .

Christ the King

Sunday between 20 and 26 November inclusive

———

Jeremiah 23. 1–6 : Ps. 46 : Colossians 1. 11–20 : Luke 23. 33–43

To you, O Christ our King and our God, belongs all power, dominion and authority in heaven and on earth. Come, rule in our hearts, help us to forward your kingdom on earth. We ask this in your holy name, Jesus Christ our Lord, living and reigning with the Father and the Holy Spirit, one God, for ever and ever. **Amen.**

You are the King of Glory, the eternal Son of the Father;
we give you praise for you have conquered the darkness of
   death and opened the kingdom of heaven to all believers.
We offer you our obedience, we give you our love, and seek to
   live to your glory.
Lord, grant that your church may be an instrument for the
   coming of your kingdom on earth.
We pray for all who are seeking to bring peace and good will to
   the earth.

May your kingdom come
in us as in heaven.

We pray for the rulers of nations and people, that they may be
open to your will and govern with grace.
We remember all who are striving for freedom, all who are
seeking to improve our world, all working to relieve poverty.
We look for the day when the kingdoms of this world will be
the kingdom of Christ.
We pray for creators of beauty, all artists and craftspeople,
musicians, sculptors, architects and gardeners.
May your kingdom come
in us as in heaven.

Lord, come and rule in our homes;
come rule in our lives and all our relationships;
come rule in all our dealings;
come rule in our hearts.
Come, Lord, change us and we shall be changed.
May your kingdom come
in us as in heaven.

We ask your blessing on all divided peoples, all suffering from
war or oppression.
We remember all who are struggling and cannot cope on their
own.
Lord, give comfort and strength to all who are ill, all who are
fearful.
We pray for friends and loved ones who are in need at this time.
May your kingdom come
in us as in heaven.

You, King of Glory, have triumphed over death,
you have defeated darkness,
you have redeemed us by love.
We commend to you all our loved ones and friends who have
departed this life.

May your kingdom come
in us as in heaven.

Let the King of Kings rule in your heart and fill you with peace.
The peace of the Lord be always with you
and also with you.

THE BLESSING

Rejoice that the Lord is King.
Serve the Saviour with gladness and love,
seek his will in all that you do,
confess him as Lord, praising his holy name;
and the blessing...

.